Star City

JOHN GALLAS was born in 1950 in Wellington, New Zealand. He came to England in 1971 and currently works for the Leicestershire Student Support Service. His previous Carcanet collections include *Practical Anarchy* (1989), *Flying Carpets over Filbert Street* (1993), *Grrrrr* (1997), *Resistance is Futile* (1999) and, as editor, the anthology of World Poetry *The Song Atlas* (2002).

T0167432

Also by John Gallas from Carcanet
Flying Carpets over Filbert Street
Grrrrr
Practical Anarchy
Resistance is Futile

As editor
The Song Atlas: A Book of World Poetry

JOHN GALLAS

Star City

Start where you are
and ask at every turn
and you will get to Star City

CARCANET

Acknowledgements

Sonnets from *The Coalville Divan* have been previously published in *The Fiddlehead*, *Stand*, *Orbis*, *The Coffee House*, *Outposts*, *Envoi*, *The Rialto*, *Poetry Ireland*, *Fortnight*, *Poetry London Newsletter*, *The Anglo-Scandinavian Journal*, *Wascana Review* and *PN Review*.

Poems from *Excellent Men* have been previously published in *Stand*, *Staple*, *Sport* (NZ), *Poetry Review* and *PN Review*.

First published in Great Britain in 2004 by
Carcanet Press Limited
Alliance House
Cross Street
Manchester M2 7AQ

Copyright © John Gallas 2004

The right of John Gallas to be identified as the author of this work
has been asserted by him in accordance with the Copyright, Designs
and Patents Act of 1988
All rights reserved

A CIP catalogue record for this book is available from the British Library
ISBN 1 85754 743 8
The publisher acknowledges financial assistance from
Arts Council England

Typeset in Monotype Bembo by XL Publishing Services, Tiverton
Printed and bound in England by SRP Ltd, Exeter

Contents

The Coalville Divan

Excellent Men

The Coalville Divan

These one hundred sonnets use as their beginnings Persian Proverbs from the *Wisdom of the East* series by L.P. Elwell-Sutton (John Murray, 1954).

Kansas Sonnet

whatever fortune awaits, let it come at once

Today a glowglass moon, all cut and thin,
snagged the early Kansas–cotton sky
and let the storm out. Jesus! Me and Ty
hid behind the Combi-Freeze. The kitchen
skattled like a bucket full of spits.
We watched the lightning lash our barren bed.
The roosters screamed, the dogies dropped down dead.
We prayed while twisters blew the barn to bits:
Oh Lord, if you was after Ty and me
for something that we done, forgive us please –
or kill us quick. Ay-men. The neighbour trees
are busted black as far as Cherokee.
Thunder whispers. Crows hop on the gate.
We sow and reap: we plough the fields and wait.

Vukovar Sonnet

trouble either passes, or comes back double

The Public Swimming Pool at Vukovar
glimmered with a flibble-flabble fizz.
Inside, the Chyernobogs, pumped up with whizz,
rocked the bride. I played my blue guitar:
the deep end danced till daylight flooded in.
The shower plipped. They took my pain away.
I told the Sergeant: 'Go tomorrow! Play
some *happy* songs.' He grabbed his violin
and fled along the ruined, moonlit street.
They left his pain and gave him mine as well:
he spoiled their funeral. A broken bell
bashes like a tocsin – *Life is Sweet!*
To get what you deserve is luck: the night
is warm, the hills are edged with bloody light.

Hunafloi Sonnet

don't shelter from the rain under a drainpipe

The seaward wind at Hunafloi is flat
and *fast*, and brings a blind of clouds. The sheep,
like little whirring combers, bowed asleep
here and there across the fields. My hat
clattered like a hovercraft and *crash!*
I bounced off down the hill. I grabbed the dog.
We landed in St Olav's porch. The fog
went *brrrr*. The gutterpipes went splish-a-splash
and splish-a-splash – and *whoosh!* The whole Saint's sea
came tubing out at us like Noah's Flood.
Shivering souls, we waited in the mud,
and missed its misty meaning, and our tea.
Hit me with the whole wide world again!
But, dear God, give me wisdom, and not rain.

Verona Sonnet

he looked at the heavens and fell into the pit

I pfutter down the Via del Lavoro.
Cement-dust shimmers in a gorgeous cone
yawning from my headlamp; stacks of veinstone;
concrete-mixers grave like lions; a glow
of barley-twisting rods; a neon tube
duels with itself. My headlamp stirs
the half-hoist block of flats. The Vespa whirrs.
The strut-crowned rooms sail bravely, cube by cube,
away. My eyes are full of tears. Maybe…
if I work hard… and save… We pfutter back.
The Vespa disappears: the world goes black.
Ker-ASH! The roadworks eat our vanity.
The Vespa sighs, the moon turns on its light:
we won't be going very far tonight.

Leicester Sonnet

he missed the thief, but found the fortune-teller

We come home in a taxi from the Club:
some twat had robbed the telly. Me and Dilim
done a line. 'So catch the cunt and killim.'
Dilim done his pigtail. Down the pub
this Monsell joey says this fuckbleach lad
were selling stash for acid up in Brady's.
Dilim chips him tripping in the Ladies,
grinning like a bastard. So we had
another line and crashed at Dilim's gran's.
She done our tealeaves: 'Rak, you godda key:
that means you get robbed.' She smiles at me.
The sun's well bright. 'And Dilim's god two fans.'
That means Make a Fucking Big Decision.
We went up school and taxed their television.

El Transito Sonnet

*God! You haven't the power to give me a donkey, but you're
powerful enough to kill me*

We left El Transito at dawn: the snow
salt-stiff and bright like pearl. Ugo went first,
quoited in a tyre. His fat lips burst
at every pant. Then me, cigar and slow,
our battery on my back. We climbed the road.
My boots bit stair by stair in Ugo's slots:
I huffed and puffed. My heart throbbed up in knots.
Then Ugo stopped. '*God help me!*' But it snowed
indifference. Ugo yelled, '*Then strike me down!*'
We heard plink-plinks of ice – a drumroll – *rocks!*
We hugged the tyre and slapped like shuttlecocks
with snowball bats and boulders back to town.
I brought him grapes. I sat on Ugo's bed.
His plasters creaked. 'He answered once,' he said.

5

Isfahan Sonnet

of all the prophets, said the mouse, you would choose Jerjis

We are Persian: lilac, shagpile, hot,
sharp, fat: along the funduq wall
we piss the burning roses, caterwaul
and kak; sulphur-spun between the kumquat
and the bergamot: sunslashed eyes
flick in fatal drowses. Soft-shit mouse
that gnaws the moonlight suq, squeakspit, squitlouse,
snip-snap! Good. The Imam's perfect lovecries
spiral up the brittle blue; and we pray
Jerjis, Jerjis, Jerjis – shut-tooth prophet,
safe to say and keep our prey: split,
sorted, sniffed. We wash and waft away.
Moonlight paints the roses. We are full.
Lilac, drowsy, fat, clever, cool.

Poti Sonnet

where there's a stone, a lame foot will find it

I bust my leg in Poti, right? we've *battered*
Boys Club Rockets forty-seven-ten
I'm *flying* on my Nike Airs right? and then
I've *whipped* this dumpshot in and *bang!* I've shattered
half my ankle right? *my shoes've burst.*
I come back two weeks later for my kit
I'm rubbish on my crutches right? I've hit
the double-doors I've started stopped reversed
I've smacked the punchbag *whack!* then it's smacked me
I've hopped and bounced and wobbled right? I've chipped
across the polished gymfloor right? I've slipped
and down I've went *I've broke my bloody knee.*
Bad Luck brings his joeys. Sochi High
won the Big Hoop Trophy. God knows why.

Baracoa Sonnet

a drowning man isn't troubled by rain

The pleasure-boat that gave me none has passed:
its bright propellers' stouty swirl withdraws
with fitful beat; the deep, like two closed doors,
is dark and bars the upward way. At last,
reversed in every blue desire to rise,
I sink more surely down than I had heart
to dare for. They are gone now. Shall I start,
so late, the selfish struggle to be wise?
Not now, when far above I hear the rain,
whose distant whisper worries me no more,
like wind on someone else's roof. What for?
The tender blue turns black and drowns my pain.
The last-loosed bubble leaves me: jelly-bright,
it falls in hurried hope towards the light.

Memba Sonnet

a stick has two ends

'… dark cafe days,' sings Joni Mitchell – 'plink.'
Me and Henry roar round Freedom Park,
blasting out the music. DJ Mark
comes on: 'It's ten o'clock!' he yells. *Blink-blink*,
an indicator pokes its nose out. 'Go!
A space!' screams Henry. 'Time' – we all join in –
'for CASH FOR CARS!' A chromey gangsta Citröen
lumbers out. 'The winner is … a yellow …
Golf three nine …' – we back up faster – 'two –
five six four two!' 'It's us!!' screams Henry. *CRASH!*
The hot dust swirls. We turn around. 'It's CASH
FOR CARSzzzzzz…' *Plink-plink*. We hit the Memba Crew.
We got a week: we met in Blenk's Motel.
They took our prize, and Henry's Golf as well.

Shizuishan Sonnet

the arrow that has left the bow never returns

They locked me up in Shizuishan. I smell
my days like some great river strung with lights
and rotted willow-green: I hear my nights
like trains whose demon clangs discord that Hell
where we who changed our minds too late are bound.
Between the barrel and his heart no prayer
of mine could stop its rush. I feel the air
rip up like cellophane: I see the sound
of threads of cotton cracked apart: and someone's
skin, that dumbly dents. I taste the ashes
we who wait are fed. The night-train crashes
through the morning, where the river runs.
They told me it was spring. My pulse is strong.
This place is always dark, and life is long.

Patmos Sonnet

he who puffs at the lamp of god will singe his beard

Boris watches. Corkscrew shreds of sea,
all firework-white, swirl up and rip: the rest –
so black – like minus. Gleb, his forehead pressed
amongst his fingers, prays in space. We three,
our bottles bright with apophatic crowns,
must find and fail our God tonight. Drink up.
The candle-nib writes wings inside my cup –
but who reads love? The moon yawns. Boris frowns
and shuts the shutters shut. Dear yellow walls,
why know why try why *hic* why not no doubt:
bind my beard and blow the candle out.
The sun is up: the first sweet seagull calls.
We puff the fiery finger one by one,
and burn our Bernard Shaws. Thy Will Be Done.

8

Dzüünbayan Sonnet

a child may hit the target in error

We galloped into Dzüünbayan, our caps
on fire with ribbons, Nobat's glasses beaming
bright as headlights. Heroes Park was teeming,
hot with hopefuls, dungsquash, bragwhoops, bowslaps,
dust and dreams. We hupped some vodkas. *Ssssh!*
Small and still, the low-stacked prize-rings sat
a hundred yards away. The homeboys, fat
and dressed to kill, went one by one. *Swish-swish* –
the arrows – *thump!* and *thump!* The Saynshand skinheads
twanged off next: then Nobat … squinting … whoooooaa …
hooooold … and *fire!* The wind went *wham!* The arrow
skewed off round the Park – and hit the reds!
Nobat won the day! We galloped back
ablaze with Right Intentions – and a yak.

Abergavenny Sonnet

blessings on the first grave-robber!

Inspector Goode appraised a vacant hole
and tipped his brogue-toe wraptly in the mud.
'We got him, boyos': one lead wisp of blood
between the O and U of 'May Her Soul' …
A housefly scaled the Usher. 'Gwillam Brown;
God may yet forgive you: I cannot.'
It squelched across the Bench; the wood was hot
and thawed its varnish. 'Four years. Take him down' …
*The coffin lid had burst: the corpse was sliced
aroundways, like a helter-skelter; strips
of rotted satin glimmered on its lips.*
'We've got a new one, boyos.' Jesus Christ.
Thank God for Gwillam Brown: corruption first,
damnation after. Bad is not the worst.

Mataram Sonnet

I'll eat what I've paid for no matter how much it croaks

Me and Weewak's sitting up the bar
in Mataram. The garden awning's broke,
the emerald monsoon's hissing in my Coke
and Weewak's *buzzing*. Then we see this car
come steaming up the hill. This geek gets out.
He goes in Bobby's Mart. The palmleaves splot.
We wait a minute. Out he comes. He's got
a Bobby's Chicken Chub. He's just about
to stuff it up his entrance when – *hang on!* –
this little emerald frog goes *whok*. He stops.
His eyeball turns. The little fella hops
along his Chicken Chub and *GOBBLE*. Gone.
'Weewak! Wow!' I gulp my khaki fizz.
I paid for it, and Weewak's wept in his.

Vel't Sonnet

he most values safety who experiences danger

Our ice Illyushin burbles over Vel't.
The flat, collapsing sun, whose bloodied scrawls
scrabble mute outside my window, falls
and cracks in freezing shreds. I drag my seatbelt
tight. The windows thrum. I just can't look.
The engines slash the great white air. We drop.
We bounce together – *bang!* – and bellyflop
on wind-planed ledges. Ivan reads his book
and giggles: pricks against the universe.
My throat blobs over. *God*. I lock my eyes.
We rake through Hell and I apologise.
Ivan smiles: Afghanistan was worse.
It landed safe. We bought a week of beer
and alchemised my wasted hours of fear.

Bucharest Sonnet

a broken hand works, but not a broken heart

Like chocolate churches crowding at the gates
of Heaven, fluffed with sweetness but no light,
unboxed, unbridled, bomb-plump, mocha-white
and hollow, skiffed in fluted paper plates
along the blue production line, my see
of Mallow Puffs go jostling at their roll
of silent cellophane. My empty soul,
unplenished by my broken heart, is free
in some unwanted way. He's gone. My hands
refuse to work. The plastic squeals and splits.
I watch them break. The Line Director sits
behind the mallow churn. She understands.
I dreamed last night that Heaven fell apart:
I used the time off work to mend my heart.

Tizoc Sonnet

escape may lie between this moment and that

'Trembling weevils – *'shun!*' A Tizoc moon
balanced gold across the lapis pillow
of the night. Captain Armadillo
clattered close and slung his tongue-harpoon
amongst the rustling, squeaky pack: a snack
before the dark patrol. *Swish! Swosh!*
Hernando! Lola! Bristling like a car-wash
he advanced on *me*. I squiggled back
and shrank in Don Pepito's wings. He shot:
I ducked: he rattled. Whew. He cranked his head
above the moonlight dust and glared. 'You're *dead.*'
A lorry squashed him like a coffeepot.
We live until we don't. We whirred away
towards the gilded sun. Another day.

Nelson Forks Sonnet

may God bless us with such enemies!

I bought a bull in Nelson Forks. Some bastard
tailed me home. I parked the pickup quick.
The bitches whined and tugged their chains. A Buick
bumped across the pumpkin field. I hid
in Burger's barn. A beat-up yellow truck
followed – bump, bump. They stopped. The sun
burned through a scarf of mist. I got my gun.
They both got out. The bitches growled. I snuck
towards the bullpen. Ssssh. They waved their arms.
The fat one crossed the frost and something popped.
The tall one furled and fell. The fat one dropped.
Echoes gonged across the frozen farms.
The police said Did I know them? I said No.
They zipped them up. The furrows filled with snow.

Samarkand Sonnet

a man with a lucky star may do as he likes

'A half of –' Earthquake! *CRASH!* The Dairy Hall
caved in and crashed. A buckled, fatful bowl
of goats-cheese sploshed my shirt. A hot blue hole
punched in from Heaven opened like an eyeball
up above. The silver sinks went bang
and all the wet white counters crawled with cracks
and shed their spotless skins like snow on sacks
of seeping curds. Beneath the shattered prang
of concrete beams and rustrods, Bulbul's hand
stiffened out to pay me. Then he died.
Now my swish apartment gleams beside
the empty, turquoise heads of Samarkand.
I kill for money. I'm a millionaire.
People say I'm lucky. I don't care.

Tougan Sonnet

when a hundred comes, ninety is here as well

I wake up good. I crank the shutters up.
I see the ladies. *Whoh!* I bop along
the coloured cotton bolts. My favourite song
chugs the windows. Life is sweet. *'Hup-hup!'*
THWONK! Mr Misery Noko's camel
folds and flops outside. Oh man. He farts.
Not the camel. Spit spit spit. He starts
to finger up the drabby drums of twill.
'Two metres eighty-four' (?) So I unwind it –
and cut him three. Why not? I'm sweet. His head
cocks up. *'Two metres eighty-four I said!'*
I hold it up. 'It's there! *Just bloody find it!'*
Shells have nuts and days have hours. He bust
my nose. The ladies sashay through the dust.

Bladgrond Sonnet

youth is its own brightness

Limpid, languid days they were, that run
away so quick, removing on their rounds
my sudden youth: sweetwhisper, hot-kop sounds,
hid shrikes and popping pods, the slow-bomb sun
and whiffling oatgrass ten foot high, and red
spit-fires and stars and miles of crapless dark.
I seen a boomslang hang his question-mark
in Bladgrond Bush, godgleam and sapphire head,
observing out a beantree through the rain.
I mended up a man. I swish the hose
across our dirty lawn: its drug-green shadows
nudge some distant venom through my brain.
I climb the kop. What happens? Even fear
is dull. I watch the cloudland disappear.

13

Warsaw Sonnet

a hurt at the right time is better than gifts at the wrong time

I watched the cornered children from my car.
I tapped my PIN. I'd seen the dog before.
I phoned upstairs. 'It's Pat.' The garage door
slid up. They kicked its head in. Caviar
and Schlitz. I tapped the lift-code. 'Anna? Pat.
I'm coming up.' The mirror shook. I tapped
the intercom. I checked my face. I wrapped
the Schlitz inside my jacket. Anna's flat
was open. She was talking on the phone.
I kissed the air. She turned around. I smiled.
Her eyes were black with pain. 'Some fucking child
just killed my dog.' I spent the night alone.
Love is free to make mistakes. I cried.
I drank the Schlitz. I phoned her up. I lied.

Nafud Sonnet

he lost a camel and went after the world

I pissed on Wadi Jizil. Skewers of sun
jabbed the pinkstone banks. I rubbed my eyes:
my camel wasn't there. A kink of flies
buzzed its dung. Zeki grabbed his gun.
We doubled up and paced across the flat
that swelled to Abu Saad. We sniffed around.
We trotted on. The moonstruck sandstone wound
its redcream lodes along the cliffs. We sat
and watched the windgrains rub our purpose thin.
We slept amongst the thorn-mats. Zeki said
the stars that glittered down at us were dead.
We reached the Nafud's edge: we galloped in.
Zeki shot a man in Wadi Khirr.
We sit and wait. I think she led us here.

Jerusalem Sonnet

not every bearded man is your father

Mmm, that's him: his cedar length cut down;
his tongue, whose salt-thyme taste I loved, laid sideways
in his cheek; his furrowed soles; the blueglaze
moons that neap his thumbnails; and his brown,
cold, atom-branching beard, not dead yet, thick
with rootless faith. I slept on Rachel's floor
and raised our child. A year shot past. The war
made other graves. And then our new-blue, public
day arrived. We took our stones. I ran
down Jaffa Road. The pramsprings squealed. I stopped.
Nathan's fingers balmed with sweat. He dropped
his stone and clutched at every bearded man.
Now he arms to face the same old dangers;
preferring, as he does, the love of strangers.

Tsu Sonnet

enjoy the fruit, but remember the tree

A thousand years ago we lived in Tsu.
The neighbours had a varnish tree that grew
against the garden wall. I never knew
it touched the earth: I only saw its blue,
elliptic leaves that shivered in the light,
the molecules of poisoned fruit, the white
wax-spikes of civet flowers, and all the bright
susurrant crown that sailed the air. One night
I climbed the wall. The paper moonlight lay
like half-hung pages through the ink X-ray
of branches. Far below my feet its grey
and corrugated pillar dived away.
Now I live alone in Shinjuku;
twenty storeys up. I like the view.

Sofia Sonnet

vinegar in hand is better than halva to come

Me and Stalin's sat in Largo Place.
It's good for business, right. I got this sign
says DESTITUTE, a can of Uzbek wine,
and Stalin's got this fucking fuck-me face
and half a pigfoot dizzied up with flies.
This blonde comes clickclack out of TsUM: she's dressed
in fifty fucking bags. I go impressed.
She sees me see her see me see. Her eyes
go guilty-good. She waves this note. She stops.
'No, no,' she goes, 'I'll get some more. The bank's –'
'I'll take it.' Stalin yaps. I grab it. 'Thanks.'
She eyes me sadly. Stalin licks his chops.
They mugged her on the steps outside St Thomas's.
Take the fucking presents, not the promises.

Jhelum Sonnet

if you have heard threats, threats will not frighten you

Dad's got flu, so I'm in charge. The *Jhelum
Hero Milling Co-op, A.I. Wazi
(Manager) and Son* – which Son is me –
rattles like a rusting-dusting drum
of talcum powder. Down my windows drifts
a haze of flour and tinkling husks that – Whoa!
What's *that?* … Ghostly white and ghastly slow,
this MONSTER noses round the shed and lifts
a bin-lid. *Munch.* So what would daddy do?
This. I rattled down the stairs. I grabbed
the hopper-tops. I *snarled.* I *bobbed.* I *jabbed.*
I *weaved.* I *yelled.* I *clattered.* Nothing. *BOO!*
Turns out the camel used to carry flak
to Kabul. I got sick-leave. Dad came back.

Marañon Sonnet

words are not arrows

I blabbled by the Marañon. I steamed
and scratched and stretched my little snout towards
the sun, that blobbed and blinked the bubbly swards
of yellow-popping jesusweed, and beamed
around my bosky bed. The fat macaws
snored. Across the amber *agua* floated
Baby Boa's bilious hiss: 'Yew bloated,
blubbered sssslime-balloon' – I licked my paws –
'Yew ssssewer-sssssucking sssssack of ssssscabs, yew turd,
yew nerd' – I twirled my tail. The sun still shone
its shining swirls along the Marañon.
So who was ever eaten by a word?
I whisk my whiskers. Darkness dulls the trees.
The water swishes. Pooh – it's just the breeze.

Dundalk Sonnet

if you die for someone, make sure he has a fever for you

I'm dying for King Billy ain't I Sam?
The rain is raw, the earth is dim and dreary.
My cheeks are pale, my heart is weak and weary.
I'm dying for King Billy ain't I Sam?
Tell him how I struggled won't you Sam?
The sun is dark, the fields are black with mud.
My rifle's broke, my britches drip with blood.
Tell him how I struggled won't you Sam?
Whisper what he told you will you Sam?
He's lying with a fever in Kilkee.
Don't you think King Billy's sick for me?
Whisper what he told you won't you Sam?
Wake me when you hear King Billy's drums.
Hold me to Attention when he comes.

17

Würzburg Sonnet

every man's beliefs provoke another to oppose them

The sleep syringe decants its spike of breath:
the surgeon takes my hands. I miss the way
you feel. While Plotzschen feeds me off my tray
I calculate the fraction of my death.
My fingers frisk your spine; the Pfeffers gush
their stinking cigarillos while we sing
the Waffen SS song: Röntgenring
is shot with moonlight. Plotzschen shivers – Hush.
I raise my hands of air: the bullets shred
each one, a stick along my railings. You,
in that decelerated atom, knew
how little flesh was wise, and lost your head.
Plotzschen smiles. The windows prick with rain.
The blue syringe decants its dreams again.

Karakaya Sonnet

a great river may be dammed at its source with a stick

The wind wound down from Hindi Baba, torn
on skerries, blue with sleep. I flicked the paper:
Bears in Bitlis. Sheets of fizzy vapour
rustled round the windows. Yawn yawn yawn.
I sat astride the wide Euphrates, dammed
beneath my blinking meters. *Konya 3 –*
Malatya 1. I swirled and sucked my tea.
The TVs flicked, unmoved. A side-door slammed.
Bang! I dropped my teaglass. Nothing. But …
I could have touched his sleeve. His eyes were full
of faith. I watched him, dream-deliberate, pull
the burning switch that ground the spillgates shut.
From here to Abadan the river drained
like blue thread from a rug. And then it rained.

Bangassou Sonnet

war at the beginning is better than peace at the end

Before we fetch my suit from Bangassou,
me and Charlie's got a rendezvous
at Candy's Steak and Grill. I need a few
to calm me down and see this whole thing through.
I get a beer. He gets this fizzy, pink
balloon of pop. I punch him in the nose.
Before he starts. He's flushed and crushed. He blows
his hanky full of blood. ' *"You shouldn't dwink"'* –
I do his whine – ' *"and dwive"* – you piss me off –
you drive – you can't – we crash – no wedding. Right?'
He coughs a bloody, small, agreeing cough.
Strike the gathering storm before it starts,
or how could we domesticate our hearts.

Antarctic Sonnet

a thought may bring life to a desert

Whirring like the key that winds the world,
a windgauge spins its spoons in nothing white.
We wait together. Longitudes of light
shoot out like neon tubes above us, swirled
with mizzled milk. Somewhere in this place
that has no *where*, my ghost Sikorsky bores
its groundless line this way. An icy gauze
obscures my heart. I hide my frosty face
inside this space that has no sides, this bitter
no-bird Byrdland, blank, unborn, inert.
14:00 hours: *a lime-green shirt
in Trautmann's Store*. I hear the rotors clitter.
I sow the virgin snow with violet stains:
distant cures await our present pains.

Christchurch Sonnet

if you have no door, why have a doorman

We drove to Christchurch, scrubbed and slightly brave.
The T-bone steaks were big as daddy's hat.
The plates were thick and white and wet. We sat
in modest sweetness, brought up to behave
with short-sleeved hopes that set us down as hicks.
The ice-cream came in glasses. Mum declined
the paper napkins. Daddy smiled behind
his pipe-smoke. Heading back towards the sticks,
we passed the white, suburban houses crowned
with space potato-mashers: Heaven spilled
its secret buzz around them. Brightness filled
my brother's daydreams … Daddy turned around.
He winked – 'They haven't really got TVs.
They're just for show.' And Town turned into trees.

Abomey Sonnet

ask your conscience, then fleece the village

Bitten by the Wasting Flea, Boo-Kay
rippled like a muddy stream along
her yellow stretcher, fished with yellow, singsong
baits of breath that took her breath away.
I wailed while aunts and uncles shuffled through
the kitchen: sunshine scraped across the floor.
I ticked my fly-whisk. Round her wrist she wore
the useless charm I sold her: spit, bamboo
and dog's hair. So did half the village. Soon,
too strong to wait, she cooed herself away.
I caught the midnight bus to Abomey.
The gravel glittered, minted by the moon.
We sprout, we rot: so what if we should glean
a little bit of business in between.

Macduff Sonnet

what is carried away by the wind may be brought to anyone

We hae some bluidy billows roon' Macduff:
the flurry's awfie fierce that slings the spray;
the current's awfie cruel that beats the bay;
an' when they're bluidy blent it's awfie rough
to drag wee Bobbie up an' doon the shore
an' keep his puir wee paddies on the ground.
Mary Humphie's darlin' Dandy drowned
on Christmas Day; an' now the breakers roar
agin the wind an' Bobbie's marchin' hame
an' *WHACK!* he's whipped awa'. His sad wee bark
near cracked my hert. The whirlin' sky ran dark
an' stubborn still I stayed an' called his name.
Mary foond him cooried in her bed,
all stiff wi' cauld an' salt. He wasna' dead.

Tarat Sonnet

whoever wants a peacock must put up with a journey to India

My sunstroked body sucks its drip of dope;
the mirror shines me crimson on a floe
of sapstained Clinic bedding in the low
alarm of milkshake neon. Every hope
I had has sunned since I, with iron joy,
pursued the sweet intentions of my heart
towards the empty world, and reached Tarat.
It burned like innocence before a boy
who kept its photograph for thirty years
inside his wallet, self-deceived that dreams
were best unvisited. The salt-drip gleams
above my bed like undelivered tears.
My soul is high with sleep. Outside, the street
ripples with the flap of hurried feet.

Paris Sonnet

you will eat no more stew than you pay for

A scarlet box. I jammed the plywood door
and squinnied round. I combed the blowsy air.
The lightbulb blushed. A buggered metal chair.
A silver piss-pond nosed across the floor.
I wrapped a nest of tissues round my knob
and fed the meter: *Fucking on the Farm.*
He squeezed her smock. A sheep went past. My arm
refrained. A Rambouillet! I watched it bob
behind her gasping arsehole. Then it coughed
and woolled away. He sucked her cunt. I stropped
my stiff back up. It ambled back. I stopped.
The picture prickled off. My knob went soft.
The Gare du Nord distempered in the rain.
I caught the train back home to Gaillefontaine.

Mol Sonnet

a man will cross the world at the smallest hope of love

Beep. Wrrrr. Clickclack. Ssssss. 'Hello?'
Ssssss. Ssssss. Ssssss. 'It's' – crackle – 'Geet.'
Crackle. 'We could' – buzzzzz. Ssssss – 'meet.'
Ssssss. Ssssss. 'If' – crackle crackle – 'Joe?'
Umm. 'I'mchangingtrainsatLeuvenstation
halfpastfiveonTuesdaymorning'bye.'
Clickclack. Beep. The Monday midnight sky
shuddered like a fridge. Our conversation
never matched our love. Too pissed to drive,
I took my bike. The roads were swiped with ice.
It snowed. My front teeth froze. I fell off twice.
'*The next train*' – Jesus! Push me! – '*to arrive…*'
We met – still moving. 'Kiss me!' That was it.
I biked back home to Mol. The sun shone. Shit.

Hawkers Gate Sonnet

you must go alone if you cannot wait

Me and Brer we been up Devils Griddle
opal-picking. Then we got these tarts
in Schicks Hotel and mines the Queen of Hearts.
Its fifteen bob. I give her jam a diddle
then I done it up the wall and then
I go to Brers. Its number ten. Theyre sat there
smoodging on this couch. You finished Brer?
Wes hardly started mate. I go again
at six o clock. Shes whistling down his drills.
They aint done nothing yet. I drunk some jugs
and evening come. I got the jitterbugs
and rode on out towards them purple hills.
I took a dekko back on Hawkers Gate.
Its twinkling in the dark. A man dont wait

Kiribati Islands Sonnet

drops that gather one by one become a sea

We huddle in a bored, ballistic mass
and watch with dull, quiescent hope the storm
that swishes round us, whose impassive swarm
of bloomy spheres and shy, gymnastic gas
re-entertains our keen eternity.
How long have we, with such intended calm,
reviewed our tiny sky, whose fixed alarm
repeats our troubled peace: how long have we,
our neutral brothers at our backs, held out
in consummate society before
the steady sweep of order: by what law
may Heaven lie in Heaven, and in doubt.
My undiscovered brothers, take my hand:
a million islands make a promised land.

Seoul Sonnet

the works of men begin to fall as soon as they are built

The Calm Apartments gush polite applause:
so why is Mrs Liu, the architect,
(a woman I admire and respect)
so sad and troubled? While the waitress pours
our Scotch, she dabs her eyes and takes my hand.
'I'm sorry. Just a touch of *mal de tout*.'
Her little shoulders shiver sharply through
her suit. She smiles. An epaulette of sand
shifts on each. *I know the cause*: the way,
quite suddenly, she stopped and touched her hair;
the way she quizzed the sky, as if somewhere
she saw some whisper of the world's decay.
Discreetly sweet, the waitress pours more Scotch.
I smile at Mrs Liu, who winds her watch.

Djibouti Sonnet

what does not shine may be worth more than gold

The traffic inches glinting way below.
The Foreign Office cools. The night is green.
My blue projector whirrs. Across the screen
in listless joy the people come and go
like swaddled poles with lensed-up heads that draw
towards my purple smoke. The cattle follow,
surdly tuned, in black and white. The hollow,
happy eyes. The wagging windlestraw.
The perfect sky. The greyish silhouette
of camels slouching through the sun. I think:
I'll go. I stretch, and pour myself a drink.
The film flaps off. I crush my cigarette.
I lift the scarlet blind. The plane comes down.
Way below, the earth is brilliant brown.

Budapest Sonnet

soft words will get the snake out of its hiding-place

Rick were out his fucking tree with Red.
We're down the fucking Ruszwurm eating Cakes
when buzzy-buzz he gets the fucking shakes
and flings his fucking Gypsy Gingerbread
halfway up the fucking wall and CRASHes
off his chair. The Boss goes fucking mental.
Rick don't move. 'You gotta do it *gentle*.'
Everybody stares. The coffee splashes
softly off our table on the floor.
'We're going home.' I kiss him. 'Come on Rick.
We'll gerra taxi then I'll suck your dick.'
I help him up, and gently out the door.
Now he's sleeping peaceful in my bed.
Angry words are better left unsaid.

Luxembourg Sonnet

unless the child cries how will it get milk

I followed Mrs Prinz. Her lampblack Cats
squeeched across the tiles. Her sapphic smiles
spread amongst the pliant paedophiles
like hemlock, whilst the spick, contending brats
made faces in the air. She paused. A pink
kerfuffle blush; a little Mozart posed
like Meissen; and a shepherdess exposed
her onion ankles to the hall. 'I think …' –
and then a wail: so struck with age and fear,
so dreadful of the world. She chose her Queen
and held her up and smiled: Cot 17 –
The Luxembourgeois Baby of the Year.
The cameras popped. I followed Mrs Prinz
beyond the painted cribs of innocence.

Efate Sonnet

no one scratches my back but my own fingernail

Dear Sir Detective Sergeant Mr Childer,
I lived next door to Sonny Nupanai.
I think I know what happened. Last July
his house fell down. He tried to sue the builder
(Lau's Commercial, Homes & Boats) but lost.
He never trusted no one after that.
He fixed the place himself; and then he sat
inside. His sister came from Pentecost
to try and get him out. He nearly killed her.
Sonny never hurt a fly before.
He touched her, see – that's why he tried to saw
his arm off. Yours sincerely, Father Childer.
Heaven knows our neighbours: but we lie
in separate straits like islands. God knows why.

Muscat Sonnet

the master's eye has its own effect

Mohammed left his camel in my care
and flew away to Paris for the races.
Removed from all her brown, familiar places,
Faith-and-Courage pined; declined to share
her stamping ground with Bullet, my Aîr,
refused her greens and slumped with milky eyes
against the garden ditches, wreathed with flies.
I mooched around the runnels. Through the clear,
electric blue I watched his plane unload
its vapour trail. Mohammed smiled: 'I won.'
He called for Faith-and-Courage, and the sun
divined their shadows racing down the road.
Bullet sniffed and spat. The moon, a slice
of lime, hung halfway up to Paradise.

Doha Sonnet

a mother burns her heart, a nurse her apron

Fahad's gone to school. The kitchen door
is just ajar. I watch his nurse unknot
her apron, which she neatly folds. Still hot,
the stove draws off her sweat. She sweeps the floor
and takes her birdcage down. I watch her drop
the apron in: its ashy thickness keels
like withered leaves. She leaves. The budgie squeals
across the sand. They're gone. *Now burn me!* Stop
my heart, whose squeal and sweat and sentence tire
my soul. I made him. Sunlight burns the floor.
The embers ebb. I close the kitchen door
and drag the petrol-can towards the fire.
The budgie blinks. His burning birdcage swings
towards the Gulf. He fluffs his yellow wings.

Manaus Sonnet

if I'd been there she would've had a son

I picked my teeth and watched Accountant Nine.
He slit his steak and giggled. Rolls of smoke
blued above the table. Someone broke
a plate: he laughed. His breath was bent with wine.
His gellied hairslick gleamed. His serviette
was used, but neatly folded. Someone smashed
a glass: he laughed again. His pager flashed.
I watched his pupils scroll and blither. Sweat
improved his rat moustache. I waited. Someone
dropped a knife. 'My wife's just had a child.'
He stared at me. 'A girl.' He frowned. I smiled.
'If I'd been there she would have had a son.'
We offered him the job. He turned it down.
We meet each other now and then in town.

Kikwit Sonnet

he who has to sit and wait for his friend will sleep hungry

Du's my bruvver, man. We been togever
time. He ain't done nuffing I ain't done:
I ain't done nuffing he ain't done. Cept one.
He's went away to Kikwit, an I never.
Then I just done nuffing. Now I caught
the bus. We got this magic, man, I'll find him
easy like I use to walk behind him
through the bush. This town ain't like I thought.
This here's his door; but I ain't got the key.
The sun goes falling down the dust, the moon
comes shining up the dark. He's coming soon.
I squat against his doorstep. Wait and see.
The stars hang up their lights. We use to lie
in bunks of dust an ride them through the sky.

Kvænangen Sonnet

without society, a man may think what he will

I paid a lot. It's worth it. From my lawn
the fjord's long, haunted hall of drizzle fades
between the hills, whose chest-deep army wades,
like giants, into space. My heart is drawn
in black and white behind some sail that seeks
the earth's bright edge; and far above the geese,
like ghosts of better men, distil my peace
in passing. No one comes here. Orange streaks
of sunset blaze the rocks. The sea is white,
and swells like rippled lead. This age is dead:
I wait for heroes. When the sky turns red
and bloods my roof, I go inside and write.
The drizzle drifts. The stars are cold and clear.
The keyboard rattles. Nothing stops me here.

Mut Sonnet

he who eats the bread of his hands has no need of generosity

That skiting bastard Abduh Maqsoud Zati
bobbled up the mudbank on his neddy.
'*Yo! Poor people! Yo! Respect! You ready?*'
No. '*You hungry?*' No. '*You wanna party?*'
No. He knocked his knock. I let him in.
He kept his shades on. Insects sucked his jeans.
He strutted round the room. A tin of beans
rattled in the fireplace. '*You look thin.*'
I spat. '*I'm getting married.*' 'Really? Why?'
His lips, like sweating raisins, creased with light:
'*You coming?*' 'This is all I need tonight':
I wagged my fist. The bean tin bubbled dry.
He bobbled off to Mut. '*Poor people! Yo!
Respect!*' And wore away. '*You hungry?*' No.

Qamdo Sonnet

to die with honour is better than to live with disgrace

Zigzag crackles shotgunned out of space:
Little Hoo sat bleeding in the grass.
The river ramped beside him, raw as glass.
I saw a drop drop in, as if the face
of Namcha Barwa flapped with scarlet cloth.
I wiped my glasses. Freedom never cost
so much. He rocked and whispered. Loosening frost
dribbled down his neck. A belt of froth
blacked his pants. His arms, held out against me,
shook and strained and shivered, shocked that I,
to buy him books, had practised in Shanghai.
He drained without a murmur. I was free.
I ditched my kit. The dressings swirled and sank.
I took his boots. They burned him on the bank.

Bourail Sonnet

good deeds return to the house of their author

I coughed all night. The pillows stank with sweat.
At two o'clock I drooped downstairs and sucked
some lemons on the lawn. The chickens clucked.
The moon–Pacific sliced the silhouette
of Madam Mumu's fence from purple paper.
Spicy bushes breathed … I took a deep –
COUGH-COUGH! I crawled upstairs. I fell asleep.
But not for long. A misty, wispy vapour
corkscrewed through the roof. A tiny boat
spiralled down its purple coil. *COUGH-COUGH!*
The chickens squawked. I threw the covers off.
The bumboat whooped and vanished down my throat.
I woke at twelve o'clock. The white sea shone
across my sweaty sheets. My cough was gone.

Port Louis Sonnet

hate cannot be washed out with blood

I squeezed my juice. He scorched his best white shirt.
He flipped. He took the Jeep and roared away.
I chased him. Near the turn for Tombeau Bay
I clipped a pig. I stopped. I wasn't hurt.
But Angel … did some trick of hate distract
his heart? He glanced behind. He swerved. He crashed.
His blood ran out the door. The wipers slashed
his neck. I hold his hand. His plasters, cracked
and quickly cast, are touched with dents. Above,
the borrowed-blood-bag drips. Perhaps his heart,
new-filled, new-driven, fired and flushed will start,
again, at last, a straighter branch of love.
The crimson needle ticks. His pulse is stronger.
Jesus, let him sleep a little longer.

Arros Sonnet

a passing shadow doesn't make eternal night

The forest flapped. *Biff … Boff … Thud*:
pinecones bombed the mould. Amidst the gloom,
hunched in creaking everdarks, a doom
of mother vultures phlegmed their raddled cud
and rocked, with hooded joy, their snapping eggs.
Something dimmed the wind. The mothers wound
their necks erect and hissed. It swooped around
the treetops: '*Hide your babies!*' Tiny legs
stabbed the shelltops. Something sliced the sky.
Señora Airsteak stropped her claws. The others
blinked … the wind died down… The gargling mothers
cranked their wings across their ogled fry.
A lime balloonist drifted down the hill
towards Arros. The woods lay hushed and still.

Stockholm Sonnet

finish off your enemy before you celebrate

Greta Yacht-Ears, Baby-Sitter, smirked.
She eyed my cool, convincing snooze and snuck
towards the fridge. '*I WEREN'T ASLEEP!*' 'Oh *fuck*.'
She dropped a can of mummy's beer. It blurked
across our shagpile rug. She grinned like sick.
I bongoed off the couch: she bounced me back.
I done kyokushinkai: *whack-whack-whack!*
She pinned me down. She Ommed me. What a prick.
I Ommed her back. 'G-goooo to sleeeeeep.' Her head
went bobble-wobble. Wicked. '*Gooooo to sleeeeeeep.*'
She went. I drank mum's beer. I made a heap
of empties round the couch and went to bed.
Mummy chucked her out. I had a piss
and waited for my second goodnight kiss.

Port-de-Paix Sonnet

the farmer sees rain in the sky, the washerwoman sun

I dream of drizzle … Cockadoodledoo!
The sun roils up. It climbs the clapperboards
and burns across our bed. I turn towards
my other whale and watch the welling dew
tattoo her great, cool skin with signs of sweat.
Her nipples drip. Our stomachs softly fight,
and suddenly her hair explodes with light
and crinkles. Half my arse is white and wet.
Yesterday the cane turned brown: today
the sky is streaked with gauzy clouds. She smiles.
'I hope it's fine.' }
'I hope it rains.' } we say together. Miles
of washing ruffle down to Port-de-Paix.
Everything is someone's wish. She slides
against my heartbeat while the day decides.

Notia Sonnet

the goat dreams one thing, the goat-herd another

I snuggle up to Hercules. The storm
tunes up between the trees. The furnace blinks
like sleepy chooks. He shakes his dags. He stinks.
I gulp some hooch and yawn. At least he's warm.
The fields lie dead outside: why can't *I* dream
till spring? The shutters squeal. Tonight will do.
I snuggle up to Man-Who-Frowns. I chew
his tasteless pants. The scrumptious bushes scream
outside. I kick his head: he snorts. The storm
engulfs my greens and pops the sun, which blinks
across the room. He slops his jug. He stinks.
I hoist my horns and yawn. At least he's warm.
He dreams of women, death and nothing done,
and billy dreams of dozing in the sun.

Vienna Sonnet

even a pimple may change the course of love

I've got this spot: it sticks up like a wigwam
in my face. St Wolfgang's goldly gleams.
I sing. I pray. I burn. My plook blasphemes
the glass-stained gasps of Glory. *Damn, damn, damn!*
She sits, half-hid, across the aisle. Each prayer
permits her kneeling, knowing peek. Last week
I answered with my eyes: but now my cheek,
whose pus-distempered horn provokes the stare
of every striving Christian heart, withdraws
from Love behind my pew. The organ swells:
I shrink with fierce devotion, and the bells
bang bravely as she tiptoes out the doors.
And now it's gone, she never comes. I smile,
unspotted, at her seat across the aisle.

Catamarca Sonnet

facts have reasons

'Diego Luis Quinto Abejon?'
I cackled in my cups. 'Doan make me laugh.'
The hacks went 'O?' His half-drawn epitaph,
'*The Curtain King of Catamarca*', shone
like satin off the iMac. 'Well ...' – I smiled –
'He spent the War in Texas – *selling corn.*'
They smoked like trains and whistled. 'He was born –
inNegroMuerto!' 'What?' 'He – hic – *defiled* –
theLeninSisters!!!' 'Jesus Christ!!' 'He shot –
FranciscoDiamondPico!!!' Fuck!!! 'Last week –
hesackedme!!!!' Silence. 'Hic.' A little leak
of sherry lapped my collar: *dot dot dot ...*
They took the bottle back. I dabbed my eyes.
The keyboard clicked. They filled the screen with lies.

Kala Oya Sonnet

the camel-driver reaps where the muleteer sowed

We saw them coming, small at first, like midges,
through the rice. We stayed our hoes and watched.
They grew to men. Their teakish faces, blotched
and breathless, nodded up the half-dug ridges,
warping all the air, that gleamed like ghee.
The chickens throbbed, their hearts blown up with heat.
We waited. Could this Glorious Retreat
restore my dutied son? We took them tea.
They quizzed our faith in Faith. Their faces gleamed
with sweat. But no one knew his name. They ate
my chickens, every one, to demonstrate
my grey Belief in theirs. The paddies steamed.
We watched them go like Freedom through the rain:
we heaved our hoes and fought the fields again.

Bangkok Sonnet

rage seeks a whipping-boy

Remember Ban Mong Pong? The house; the hill;
and all the green beginnings of our lives?
Amidst this coil some whispered hope survives
to bait my heart with discontent, and kill
its dry begetter. Ratcha Damri Drive
distils the rage of fifty thousand cars
that cannot move. I clamour at the stars
behind my oily windows. Half past five.
What hope have I against such spite? Still red,
still red … *The midnight moonlight creams the floor.*
He's sleeping now. I softly shut the door.
My rest, my comfort. Blood disturbs the bed.
I drive back home. The roads are cool and clear.
My foolish disappointments disappear.

34

Binh Gia Sonnet

money goes to one place, suspicion to a thousand

I told the police my goat were pinched last night.
They said Haha, you keep your eyes peeled sonny:
write down what you seen. I seen some funny
things. I keep real quiet. Then I write:
New big hairy rug at Mrs Doc's.
Le Kim Nhan wear slippers. Grass got cut
at Phung Van Tin's. Red Chicken Restront shut.
Chews in Hong Hai's jacket. Lan Ly locks
his woodshed. Bones in Tran Duy Bach Mai's bin.
Sugar got red trousers. Yellow silk
hang in Vu Khac Xuyen's windows. Milk
in Baby Chau Dung's bottle. Signed, N. Chin.
I show them what I write. Haha, they go:
suspicion makes the world a thief. I know.

Ascension Sonnet

you can't unload the caravan for one lame donkey

It's six a.m. We're swarming up a drain.
Someone up the front knows what we're doing.
Me and Tich are flying up the flueing.
Snap! My leg falls off. You can't complain:
you can't expect an army on the trail
of half a dog and sugar-sick to stop
and say Oh dear, Goodbye. I squirm and flop
along the gutter's edge. A wizened snail
laced up in cobwebs grins across the slime.
I hear a million footsteps fading. *Tich!*
The sun smacks like a snare-drum. Life's a bitch.
My head goes dry. I'm running out of Time.
I climb a twig to face the Ant Unknown.
We have to face our last few pricks alone.

Split Sonnet

a stranger's succour pleases God

Ziggy Bendo's bitch attacked my legs.
I got this morbid twitch. I had a fit.
Mum sat by my bed till Hadjuk Split
were drawn away at Brod; then Uncle Dregs
took over till he had to go to work,
so Erno, who's my mum's half-brother's son,
came in from half past twelve to half past one,
and left his grandad's nephew, who's a Turk,
standing like a mighty tree above
my sweaty, scrunched divan. And when I woke,
refreshed and pink, this little hairy bloke
I'd never seen before said, 'God is Love.'
I thank you all for such sweet sympathy:
in comforting the world, you comfort me.

Vila do Conde Sonnet

he dedicated spilt oil to the shrine

I drop my pearly seashells in the dish
and whisper, '*Please forgive my sins.*' The Virgin
smiles amidst her candle-trill, a Sturgeon
pressed against her Breast. A frieze of fish
circumnavigates the altar-rail.
I bow away amongst the shady pews
and knot my net. A man comes in. His shoes
caress the tiles. He kneels and prays. His pale,
bejewelled hand corrects his Brylcreemed hair.
His bracelet snags and snaps. He frowns. He twists.
The Virgin smiles. He writhes his tangled wrists
and *clink!* it falls. The gusted tapers flare.
He drops it in the altar-dish and grins.
The Sturgeon glitters. '*Please forgive my sins.*'

Santa Tecla Sonnet

she gives a party with her bath-water

We usually drank champagne for half an hour
before she came downstairs in something black
and salsaed on a mirrorful of smack
till morning woke the walls. *I drop my flower,*
which crashes on her gilded coffin-top
and breaks its back and bleeds. And when the sun
had milked the floor she gave us, one by one,
her Morning Drink in brickish bowls. *I drop*
a clod of earth. The sad, autumnal light
divines the end of golden days. Her daughter
takes my hand and whispers, 'It was water:
the water from her bath.' She hugs me tight.
The lights of Santa Tecla fade and die.
I go inside as morning rots the sky.

Guatemala City Sonnet

the sheikh succumbed to the broth

I know he loves *Pescado Abulita*:
we'll give him that. Knock-knock. The Boss arrives.
I bow and scrape. A gin: of *course*. Our wives
kisskiss like scissors. 'Marta!' 'Carmencita!'
Good. But wait until he's blissed with fish
before I mention Money. Half past nine:
I wink the wife. Tortillas, tacos, wine –
and then the dreamy, steamy, limey dish.
His fat, wet eyes go weak. I watch him heave
three helpings down his gut. He burps and sighs.
I take my chance. 'Excuse me, Sir –' – his eyes
go gaga. *SPLOSH*: he pukes. She screams. They leave.
We share a cigarette and wash the floor.
He called me kin next day and gave me more.

Mumbue Sonnet

the full man knows not the hungry, or the rider the walker

I'm walkin in my feet to Mumbue.
The sun comes up. I'm cracklin like a chicken.
Man, I'm *happy*. Somethin's comin, kickin
clouds of yellow grit behin me. *Hey!*
Stop! It don't. Who cares? It belts away.
I seen inside the flyin cotton curtain:
Grief embraced the Judge. My toes are hurtin.
Man, I got to walk another *day*.
How quick they fly to sorrow! What I got
the other end improves with every dream
my limp allows me. Flamin aloes gleam
along the long horizon, fat an hot.
Whyever hurry? Happiness will keep,
an sorrow passes. Sleep, my baby, sleep.

Qurghonteppa Sonnet

there are many walnuts in the qazi's house, but they're all counted

We tiptoed through the hairbrush twang of grass
towards his house. The midnight moonlight sang
along his shutters. *Sssh. Creeeeeak – CLANG!*
We held our breaths. We tiptoed through the glass
and down the plaster passage to a door
whose name said *God is Great: His Plenty*. Yum.
We picked the lock. A forty-gallon drum
of walnuts flooded fatly on the floor.
I winked at Ek: he necked his sack. I threw
an armful in. He flashed his torch: '*Waitwait!*
There's 99 on this! What's yours got?' '8.'
'They've all been bloody *counted!*' It was true.
We tiptoed home. The minaret was white
with moonlight, like a One against the night.

Impfondo Sonnet

he smells kebabs, but it's only roasting donkey

I slap along the riverbank. The sun
distills the emerald beds of watercress,
upon whose sweet, spinacheous comfiness
I nap awhile. *Rivet*. Bullflies run
atwinkle on the creek; the breeze … I wake.
The ground goes BOOM BOOM BOOM! The bullflies flee.
Rivet! Rivet! Gulp. A trampling tree
comes trampling down the bank. The bogworts shake.
I ask an eel, 'Wharrivet?' '*MAN.*' It stands
like thunder on the shore. A man! We wait
for Music and Enlightenment: our Fate,
the Primal Puddock said, hangs in His hands.
He crouches, craps and booms off through the trees.
We blink. The bullflies blow back on the breeze.

Dhar Sonnet

a single hair from a bear is proof

My greatest triumph? Hmmm. It was a dare.
I must have been oh nine or ten. The Fair
was up in Dhar. I had to pluck a hair
from Bugger Battachariya's Boxing Bear,
witnessed by at least three Tonk Street Bros.
I climbed the tarry palings. I can smell
his sad nut-sourness now. A little bell
wrang his neck. His scabby, skewered nose
sniffsniffled upwards, like he smelt some Bear
Nirvana. Well, that's what I thought. He tried
to box his paws. I grabbed his fur. He sighed.
I ran. The Bros went mad. I got my hair.
And here it is. I showed the Bros. They smiled.
The man is sometimes smaller than the child.

Gabarone Sonnet

a miser serves his cheese in a jar

We saved his daughter. Just. The night-nurse dabs
her starveling claw. The pink drip drips. Her skin,
like paper stretched on wires; her skullet grin;
her heart: all wasted, *D.I. Moses grabs*
the hatchet. Crash! He's dead; she's in a chair,
rustling like a moth. A skid of scars
rings her palm. We found a tray of jars:
each contained one thing – a yam, a pear,
an egg, a glass of gingerbeer, a sweet,
a slice of pork, a fish, a bean, some bread.
The night-nurse pulls the curtain round her bed.
The bottle drips sedately: let her eat.
'*We only looked: he never told me why.*'
She searches through the window for the sky.

Georgetown Sonnet

God knew the donkey and wouldn't give it horns

'Oh *man*,' I say, 'You'll bust your fucking guts.'
'Fuck off,' he froths. I light a fag and smile.
My darling brother stuffs his face: a pile
of splashy goose-breasts, cream and beer. He cuts
the flesh like murder: bleeding grease, it dies.
He wipes his fresh-cut goatee. Ugh. He burps.
'More fucking beer.' It comes. I smoke. He slurps
his chocolate-cream. '*Oi – YOU!*' He stops. His eyes
coil slowly round. '*You pig-tit, murdering shit!*'
The tiny strangers slap his face and run.
'You little cunts!' He grunts. He yanks his gun.
It's stuck. Thank Christ. I crush my fag and spit.
When God made Pooks a killer, he was kind:
he also made him stupid, fat and blind.

Popakai Sonnet

when the snake is old, the frog will tease him

Is strength not made to use? Is poison meant
to sit unspat when spitting serves its kind?
Is sweet surprise a sin when God designed
our creeping shades to match our beds? Who sent
me kings to see them fall? Who gave me death
to see it wait through all this darkness? Why,
when all my nature withers, can't I die?
The grass is warm; the river sings; my breath
scrapes back and forth like leaves across a stone,
and all the short, alerted, lordless things
whose furry families feared my hugs and stings,
are dancing on my head, and I'm alone.
Like ashes waiting for the wind I lie
and watch the river snake towards the sky.

Tukums Sonnet

kindness to evil men is as bad as injury to good men

22 and 20 Chalky Pit.
I robbed the red one: all the stuff was junk.
The old guy's fast asleep. I seen this trunk
behind the sofa full of army shit.
I got these old-style medals. Tukums Fats
bought the lot for sixty fags. I done
the blue one's bathroom tiles. I seen this gun
behind the bed. He paid me twenty lats.
He don't like jews. The old guy's sat next door
shivering in the sun. 'Gidday.' 'Gidday.'
He stares. I hate this crap. I walk away.
The sky's all dust. I stop at 24.
It's dark inside. I watch the quarry cranes
swing their arms across the windowpanes.

Tyre Sonnet

when a fountain goes up, it comes down

Deep in weeds and one another's arms
we watched the Civic Fireworks over Tyre
tattoo the sky like drawings done with fire
to celebrate the Cup. Our sweet salaams
gave way to warmer greetings: Heaven fizzed,
while round us lemons *boo*ed in blooms of light,
the tractors winked, and midges pricked the night
like messages in morse. A rocket whizzed
above the farm and burst. We panted. *Crack!*
I felt the Big Thrill coming – *aah-aah*-WHAM!
It whistled down and coshed me. Midnight swam
with stars. I flopped. Then everything went black.
Said walked me gently back to town.
The streets were dancing. What goes up comes down.

Amman Sonnet

musk is known by its smell, not the shopkeeper's words

'As smooth as a sheet and as sweet as a sweet; nutritious,
delicious, delightful and sprightful and dreamy as silk;
as fat as a sausage in sassafras, creamy as milk;
a Quazi of Fishes, A Mogul of Dishes; capricious,
lubricious, the Sultan of Mambo, the Queen of the Deep;
scrumptious with camel's milk, aubergines, pickles and beans;
with anchovies, lovage-leaves, lentils and lashings of greens;
as cool as a cucumber, fragrant and filling and cheap;
unequalled, unsequelled, the Whacker, the Whopper, the Winner,
the One; stuff it or steak it or bake or boil it
or roast it or toast it or roux it or stew it or broil it
or fry it but BUY IT! I give you *THE NUMBER ONE DINNER!*'
'That one, please.' He winked: 'You like my spiel?'
'I would've bought it anyway.' An eel.

Grønnedal Sonnet

hope of any kind will do

'Tell me lies: I'm greedy for untruth.
The one about the God who loves us – why
the good die young – immortal souls – while I
decant the moonshine – love – eternal youth –
and angels, ah! my favourites.' Albie wheezed
her concertina ready while the snow
effaced the facts of Grønnedal with slow,
elliptic softness. Albie sang: I sneezed.
'The angels say' – *achoo!* – I smiled and poured
our glasses full of steam – 'that we should pray' –
the concertina bellowed – 'every day!' –
achoo! achoo! I joined in: 'Praise the Lord!'
I dreamed of angels crucified with light.
We woke up late. The world was wide and white.

Ezulwini Valley Sonnet

a tall tree is nothing to an axe

Wulu's big: brick shit-house bloody big.
He's got some scabby goats that fuck with mine.
I fixed his fridge. He's cool. We get on fine.
So when these bastards rob our Zebby's pig,
we ask him if he'll help. He says he will.
We take the van. We have a bit of luck:
Zebby finds its guts in someone's truck
parked outside the Diamond Valley Grill.
The bar's still open. Wulu nuts the door.
Inside, the RayBan Boys are pigging chips.
They stop. They stand. They snigger. Wulu tips
the bloody bags of meat across the floor.
It went so fast. They flicked away their coats
and shot him. Now I've got his bloody goats.

Umm Lahai Sonnet

if he'd had water, he'd have been a good swimmer

We stop at Umm Lahai. The stars hang fire
like boats in books that shine across the sea
in search of God. We smile and swirl our tea.
The tent-flaps flap; we lie back to admire
what Heaven is, so far from us. A screw
of dung-smoke; Ayub yawns; the camels shift
and sigh. I snooze with proper awe, adrift
in His embrace. 'I bet you never knew,'
says Abu Saud, 'that I'm the world's best swimmer.'
Sand-dunes curl like spellbound waves. He grins.
I roll up in my rug. Forgive our sins:
I hope there's room. 'Good night.' The Heavens shimmer.
Beckham crosses – *bang!* I shut my eyes.
God accommodates our happy lies.

Grozny Sonnet

a pennyworth of liver doesn't need a silver plate

The tanks rolled in, and so did winter. Ash
and ice surround what's left of town; and we,
the sad Inspectors left to oversee
the New Beginning, sit and watch the splash
of endless rain against the yawning glass
of some damp, bolted-BigWig's villa. Lunch.
We take our satin seats and smile. A bunch
of china lilies; chilly silver; brass
and Bibles; Sputnik glasses; plates from NATO;
oils of army uncles; chandeliers
and Persian rugs. We could be here for years.
The tray arrives. We share a hard potato.
No one comes but spring. The fields turn green:
unasked, unmoved, unsown, unsung, unseen.

Vava'u Sonnet   1

---

finger by finger do not take …

I get this job at O.K. Okka's Oil.
She seems OK. But then she calls the shop
and says I have to *downsize* every drop
of Okka's Extra Palm and Okka's Royal
every time I do an oily order.
Fine. OK. I do it. Two weeks later,
in she comes. She checks the Retail Data,
dip-tanks 1 to 12, the Spill Recorder,
then the, um, *Filtration Waste*. OK.
An Okka swaps the vats. She smiles and stuffs
some somethings down my pants. 'Go on,' she puffs,
'and get yourself a tart': and oils away.
She stands up in the bath. I stand up too.
I froth her hair with Okka's Palm Shampoo.

Vava'u Sonnet   2

---

lest you lose vat by vat

Profits soar. We dance in Billy's Bar
and *booboo* every night. And every day
an Okka comes and takes the *waste* away
and slips me something – Overtime (haha).
And then she calls and says she's got this deal.
We load the boat with Okka's Extra Palm
and chug towards the docks. It's nice and calm.
And then it's not. We sink. The seagulls squeal.
We ditch the vats. The boat bobs back. OK.
We've done it. Fine. She watches while a year
of stolen drops go *glob*, and disappear.
She puffs and frowns. The jetties froth with spray.
For weeks the water bubbled like shampoo.
She lies down in the sand. I lie down too.

Guanarito Sonnet

---

a small truth will wear through a thick lie

He said he'd sheared a million sheep. As if.
He stamped and spat and smouldered round the shed
like bits of Johnny Depp. 'Okay,' I said,
'Impress me.' Christ. He snatched a teggy. *Biff!*
Bang! He yanked the little, yolking chump
between his boots. He waved his dagging shears.
Oh God! Those pleading eyes! He snipped its ears;
he nicked its panting neck; he dragged its rump
across the bloody boards. I hit him. Hard.
I snatched the shears. 'Get off, you useless prick!
Just make the coffee.' Christ. I fleeced it quick
and rolled the wool. It bubbled snot and baaed.
The coffee came. He stamped and spat. I fired him.
Then I tried it. Perfect. Christ. I hired him.

Damascus Sonnet

---

every man finds his calling

'Forgive me, Ali Sheb, I never knew.
To tell the truth, I don't think you did either.'
(Soapsuds blib his fingers.) 'Take a breather!
Sit beside me, have some tea! It's true:
you never –' *CRASH!* He used to be a waiter.
Joke. He broke the plates; he dropped the trays;
he lost the bills; he took the takeaways
away; he wrecked the Eezee Percolator …
Puff… he smokes… I made him do the dishes.
Puff… he smiles… He loved it. Floods of froth
blink across our snowy tablecloth.
He toddles off. The Eezee-Master swishes.
I used to valet cars in Jericho.
Something suits you. God will let you know.

Andorra Sonnet

even the hills need company

The sun goes down: I tell more lies. Quick quick –
while shining shadows slide along the hill
like forks across a table; while I fill
your cups with indignation; while the trick
of leaving light sets fire to fields and holds
your hearts in selfish awe of your own peace;
now let me paint the paralytic lease
of nature to your gods in greens and golds
that never were – and pour another drink.
We Vote Against the Road. Whatever hate
we had of hate has gone. We smile. We wait.
And darkness comes. Unanimous. I think.
My guests go home. A dark, dissenting roar
disturbs the buried earth. I shut the door.

Zakho Sonnet

you can't pick up two melons with one hand

Zakho Market. Six a.m. E's coming.
Right on time: Big-Knock-Down-Time. 'F-fruit!
M-monster Cheap We Must Be Mad!' I oot.
E cocks is ear. E waddles up. E's umming.
Appy man. But fat. E pokes a beauty.
'How much hoff?' E grins. We'll ave some fun.
I old them up. 'T-twofertherpriyzerwun.'
'Yum,' he says. 'Too right' – I juggle – 'Fruity,
f-firm and fuller *jooce*.' E counts is money.
E's loaded up with cheapo kak already.
E tries to take is melons. 'Whoa! S-steady!'
SPLOTCH. E drops em. *SPLOTCH*. It ain't that funny.
'A lesson learned,' e says. 'Or two,' I say.
Haha. E ups is bags and ums away.

Ginger Hill Sonnet

I am the servant of my master, not of the drink

I worked for Papa X (discretion serves
the servant well) – Retired (or what you will)
for many years. We lived in Ginger Hill.
He drank a lot: politeness, habit, nerves –
who knows? His ageing guests (the two or three
who came) would join him, silent in the sun,
and drink Tokay, and nod off one by one.
And when I'd wake them up he'd smile at me
and tell me they'd been poisoned. I'd agree –
'*A wretched year,*' I'd light their cigarettes
and watch the night redeem their silhouettes
against the purple sky, and give them tea.
'I'm here,' I'd say, 'whatever Papa thinks,
to guard your reputation, not the drink's.'

Keng Lon Sonnet

shall I believe your oath, or the tail of the cock

I'm waiting in the Waiting Room… ho hum…
a spider strings a belay down the wall
to catch a bug. There's footsteps down the hall.
KER-*ASH!* The door flies open. In they come.
'Stand *up!*' I'm standing. 'Name?' 'Wong Lee.' 'Address?'
'One-four-six-two Good Luck Rise.' They smirk.
'Age?' 'Sixteen.' My heart starts pounding. 'Work?'
'Assistant Poultry Butcher.' 'Married?' 'Yes.'
They snigger. 'Where's this rooster then?' I shrug.
'I ain't done nuffing.' One goes Hawhawhaw.
'I know my rights.' Guffawguffawguffaw.
The spider gags its thread around the bug
'Shall I believe your lies?' I look all hurt.
He bellows, '*Or the rooster down your shirt?*'

Stalden Sonnet

the larger a man's roof, the more snow it collects

Europe's full. So when the Bolts arrived
all flush with *Strike It Rich!* and fancy free
and built a Disney ranch at Stalden, we,
the neighbours of its namby spread, derived
some pleasure from their subsequent bad luck.
The house went up in spring. They sat inside
and watched TV. The Alpine Garden died.
The pretty cowbell cattle ran amok
and Helmut shot them. Then they went away.
To Bali. Winter came. The snow, uncleared,
weighed down their rooves. The chimneys disappeared.
The place collapsed. They went to St Tropez.
Springtime melts the snow. The valley blooms.
I walk the dog across their ruined rooms.

Santander Sonnet

let not love stand in the way of Love

We edge around the splashing, crashing curves
that crumple, mushed with ice and disrepair,
precariously down to Santander.
The TVs thump and bump: the pickup swerves
and shudders through the slush. I yank the wheel.
I stamp the brakes. Dear God, if we get through
I'll give You one. Alberto snores. We do.
We pass a church. The white-lit lights reveal
a plaster saint with golden hair. I take
Alberto home. I sit and watch the snow
dribble down the windscreen. Should I? No.
I try to sleep, but love keeps me awake.
I see the saint, his golden hair on fire,
and televisions standing in the choir.

Holetown Sonnet

*the quarrel must have been over the rug: they stopped fighting
as soon as they had it*

OUCH! I left the Land of Nod by jet.
The air was blue with argy-bargy. *Bop!*
Bang! Biff! Boff! Whack! Whop!
'What the – ?' *Ssssh!* The squirming silhouette
of something gruesome gobbled round the lawn.
Blossom kicked me. 'Get the bastards!' 'Pardon?'
'Sort them out!' I tiptoed down the garden
wrapped in Blossom's rug. I shivered. Yawn.
Gulp. Right. '*OI!*' They stopped. The moonlight
shopped their faces. Oh. Her brothers. Famous
Holetown yobbos. 'Wicked rug,' said Seamus.
Walter smirked. They grabbed it. Brrrr. 'Ginnight.'
'Who was it?' 'Just your brothers.' 'What?' 'They said
they'd come to get your rug. Go back to bed.'

Ozero Sevan Sonnet

if the cat prays, it is a man, not God, who has taught it

Now he's dead, I'm sorry: if my prayers
are honest now, that's why. Our begging bowls
collect the rain. Oh God, do skunks have souls?
I wait amongst the holy millionaires,
unsure of Hope and Heaven. Poor old Eddy.
Credulous and cruel, the mourners climb
the godforsaken, puddled steps: this time
perhaps I'll do it right. Okay – I'm ready:
'Rest In Peace', the congregation prays
like disappointed trees. I can't. I cling
to hopes of hopeless death. They weep and sing:
I hear the echoes of our salad days –
'*I give you Sevan Joe, the Wandering Monk,
and Eddy, the Amazing, Praying Skunk!*'

Tapah Sonnet

saying 'halva halva' doesn't sweeten the mouth

'Dodie spies on cars at Pinang Pool,
where all the lovers go. She knows this man
who sits there in a Tapah Transport van,
waiting for this girl from Dodie's school.
She saw him yesterday. He had a bag
of PeeJay's Garlic Fishballs and a bunch
of onions. Would he sacrifice his lunch
for lust? He checked his watch. He had a fag.
"He couldn't wait," said Dodie darkly. "Yuk."
The lemon woods were empty. Then he sees
her moped flicking quickly through the trees.
So guess what happens.' 'What?' I stop the truck.
'He leans right back like this, and whispers *"Cakes"*
to scent his breath.' I softly hitch the brakes.

Blantyre Sonnet

my new clothes should eat the pilau

Refused admission. Speel's. On Friday night.
Apparently my clothes. Not smart enough.
Full they said. Departed in a huff.
Ate at Goldberg's. Went back Monday night.
Same fat bouncer. Wore my Paul Smith suit.
Nothing said. Nice table by the bar.
Cocktails. Hognuts. Champagne. Caviar.
Alligator steaks. Took off my suit.
Arranged it on the chair like *that* and *that*.
Spooned the food inside it. Then the drink.
Waiters looked the other way. I think
I proved my point. Paid up and took my hat.
Tipped the bouncer. Bowed at Bwana Speel.
'I think,' I said, 'the suit deserved the meal.'

Nairobi Sonnet

seek truth from a child

Sunlight flibbles palely through the trees.
We wobble Lucky's pram and watch the dogs.
Toi-tois wave their wattles: someone jogs
along the paths; the roses buzz with bees.
He's fast asleep. We start our Spot the Ball.
Bonnie ums and ahs. I wait, my pen
held up in gentle mockery ... and then
she picks the third defender. Petals fall
on Lucky's blanket. Bonnie smiles and yawns.
I sit and rock the pram. The last few cars
give way like smoke before the first few stars,
and scarlet mowers slash the burning lawns.
They're both asleep. I watch the setting sun.
Lucky licked the envelope. We won.

Envoi Sonnet

every flower has its scent

Go now, little book, and do your worst
amidst the busy world: amuse the yaks,
instruct the bushes, speed the shiny axe
of lumberjacks and slake the wombat's thirst;
enfold the fainting heart and ... maybe not.
Tickle, then, the few inclining ears
to counterfeit the buzz of several beers
and let that be enough, and be forgot.
Go now, like a Cornflakes Man-o'-War
and sink before you find the truth. Goodbye.
I made you well, but not for much. July
the 22nd, Coalville, half past four.
The world's too big; my little book's too small.
Who needs its piping comforts then? We all.

Excellent Men

John Heaney

The man there, Beckett-headed,
spare and skerry-worn – so hardly then –
is dad. Sideways at the table
with his second glass.

Light lies factual round his drink
and small as stamps on his shoe-ends.

He takes a third – arrived
to an eyebrow's thanks.
The brush. The good jacket.
It rubs like an unbird wood.

Then, with nothing past the words,
he says he doesn't like to see it,
the boxing and his sons up there,
beyond in the clamorous light.

The fourth: and the portuall uncles bark
Heaney! and Go! – branches
clacked on the tree, once, so,
and back to themselves.

One loses: one gets no enemy.
His long leg lies over the other
without the quiet kick even
of a sported heart.

His cold sons' skulls come down
the ashy carpet while others box
and sweat whips up at the neon top
with every thump thump.

Ye showed too soon, says dad, son,
and, with a fifth, lays his eye
a moment there against
the business of words.

The fierce milk lights show all
of a terrible beating –

and with a last, then,
the blows are loaded, so,
factual and spare.
Goodnight, he says, and, Home.

Pony Express Bob Haslam

bowling along and along and along
under's a backtracking blur of old scrub
scabbing the prairie the wind in its skin
druckadrack druckadrack druckadrack druckadrack

rolling along and along and along
over's a backsliding tide of old cloud
slubbing the welkin and scribbled with sparks
druckadrack druckadrack druckadrack druckadrack

poling along and along and along
go pony go pony o living o breathing
with whoses and newses bagged up in the poke
druckadrack druckadrack druckadrack druckadrack

R lay in a crib and R'll lay in a hole
ain't stopping for nothing or nobody now
druckadrack druckadrack druckadrack druckadrack
druckadrack druckadrack druckadrack druckadrack

smacking along and along and along
under's a fevering bullet-snapped bone
twanging its wrist like a cowpoke guitar
druckadrack druckadrack druckadrack druckadrack

whacking along and along and along
over's a jaw gritting round on its hinge
and an arrow inside of it crunching its teeth
druckadrack druckadrack druckadrack druckadrack

cracking along and along and along
go pony go pony o living o breathing
with us a short starburst of nerves in the dark
druckadrack druckadrack druckadrack druckadrack

R lay in a crib and R'll lay in a hole
ain't stopping for nothing or nobody now
druckadrack druckadrack druckadrack druckadrack
druckadrack druckadrack druckadrack druckadrack

Rak 1: Ballad

My love is sailing far away
across the Indian Sea;
his heart is set for Wedding Bay
and cares no more for me.

The storms of all our kissing tears
lie carelessly astern,
and though I wait a hundred years
he never will return.

Our summer hope, our love's delight,
he left without a thought,
as ships upon the morning light
sail proudly out of port.

My love is sailing far away
across the Indian Sea;
his heart is set for Wedding Bay
and cares no more for me.

The happy days will come no more
since he has proved unkind;
and weariness lies all before,
and weariness behind.

In Freedom Town when first we met
he gave his heart to me,
but hearts are quick and soon forget
their vows of constancy.

My love is sailing far away
across the Indian Sea;
his heart is set for Wedding Bay
and cares no more for me.

I dreamed I saw him standing here,
his face all pale and wrought,
and whisper *I am married, dear,*
and all we were is naught.

And now forever I'll be true
and never see you more,
so take at last my last adieu,
adieu to Freedom's shore.

My love is sailing far away
across the Indian Sea;
his heart is set for Wedding Bay
and cares no more for me.

And still I wait in Freedom Town
come sun and wind and rain;
I'd give up hope of Heaven's crown
for one sweet kiss again.

O love is sweet and love is short
and love was my delight;
and what was all has come to naught –
Goodnight, my love, Goodnight.

My love is sailing far away
across the Indian Sea;
his heart is set for Wedding Bay
and cares no more for me.

Song for the Wairua of Te Rangihaeata

Two sounds I like especially:

a soft stick-knock the flax makes –
whose sheeny blades twine their
pulled threads in untied knots
white around the white air:
washed stones and sandflies.

a soft horoeka-hiss the wave makes –
whose soft-spit heels walk on
another's back, who pricks away round
white sheeny shuttling stones:
wet grubs and fishbones.

His pa fences crack dry.
I sit under flax-flowers and watch the waves.
They walk in, white on white. A waka
lies, air-whittled, way out there like
a woodshaving on winter grass,
fishing for another this-island.

Two sights I like especially:

a seaflat white between headland and island –
a waka, way out, and blue hills further –
a cut line through water and cloud
like a flax thread on washed white sand.
The line sings, on and under a held tongue.

a blue hill, further and cut with others –
fishfin blue, whose drizzled ridges
swim with weeping, cutting the seaflat.
I sit under flax-flowers and watch
the hill sing – Like a fish, I die.

Three wet poets

Chaucer recites to his horse out of a raincoat

Springshine and rainbounce.
Clipclop through limefizz meadows
spouts an inky toke.

Donne distills a poem in a downpour

Sleet slaps and brain burns.
Limbeck lit in a cold coat.
Pelted poet-steam.

Tennyson and his pipe are surprised by a sudden storm

Be near me – wold-burst!
Whoosh! – treedump – SPLASH – pipefizz – Damn!
When my light is low.

Becketts on the beach

Scene: the beach at Donegal.
Enter Sam and Frank.
In their thirties. Lean and tall.
L – a sandy bank.

Here they pause. We hear the sea.
R – a course of rocks.
Back – a short, umbrageous tree.
Frank removes his socks.

Small, white wave at downstage R.
Upstage L – the sky.
Sam sits down. A swelling light.
Frank sits down nearby.

Pause. They smoke. A seabird wheeps
(invisible) somewhere.
Frank removes his glasses. Sleeps.
Sam in underwear.

Lights fade slowly. Sam in spot.
Mouth moves L. No sound.
Sea R glitters. Sand L hot.
Silence. Long. Profound.

A Meditation on Oort's Cloud

Good for him and good for it. I swoosh
through jams of alexanders. Up the hill
a hare gawps at the moon. The night is still,
the view is long as death. I shiver. *Shush.*
No whistle of our history of noise
unnerves me now: no brick of all its bricks
disturbs the daily dark. While starlights pricks
eternity with names, the hare enjoys
his self-reflected awe, and so do I.
It's comforting that somewhere out in space
our bright deductions wear a Dutchman's face
and roll with soul around the unmade sky.
The hare still gawps. We watch the heavens shine.
He sees his hope, and I imagine mine.

Little Ismet's Wedding

I went down on my hams in a turned Kurdish
field and pushed. A hot, glairy tube
keeled out of my innards and parked,
panting, in a furrow. I sighed carefully.

Sugared cinnabar mountains, their shoulders ranged
at weightier heights, let a cold white breath
down the ploughlines – and, gorged in ochre, the Dijle
shook my clawing toes from miles away.

I looked quietly round. My grave, polite defender,
Ismet's back, flapped, shalvar and hat.
Smoke snatched from it: a rifle as if
ran it through. Clouds butted on above.

I used my finger distantly. Water fell,
sharp, on my heels. Between field-waves
the air ran on, cold as an idea. Snow
dabbed the water-tin. I ratcheted my belt.

The hard, heartbreaking land where we were young
holds all the lime-green summer's sway.
I splashed the tin. He stared at weightier heights.
Wind piped through field and rifle-eye.

No bird. No tree. I blew my hands.
A thread of tobacco sang on Ismet's cheek.
We stumbled the earth back to his wedding
and danced The Waving Handkerchief.

Basho and his Pupils

Turquoise moon and rain.
His art pricks our untrained thoughts
each with a blue seed.

Our ginger trousers:
blossoms on the polished floor.
He bows at branches.

A nibbed cricket churrs
on a curved, stirred barley-stem:
a huge branch creaking.

He baits sharp first lines.
We flicker onto his hook.
He pulls up poems.

'*Monkeys on the roof.*'
The primacy of primates
over my study.

'*A cream spring onion.*'
The sharp taste of the master
fresh in our green mouths.

'*Three white narcissi.*'
Daughters of paper moonlight …
(Banal. Abandoned.)

Our shaved napes' hairlines.
Burnt stubble on the brain-field.
The master fires us.

Thirty-six sloe stalks
from navel to pubic hair.
Wheatfield walks reversed.

'*Sitting cross-legged.*'
Backbone-cuttings in tawn pots
inventing flowers.

Dew and goosepimples.
Morning snuffs discretion's light
and sends us to sleep.

boy in a cupboard

for Paul Sondhof, hidden there by his piano teacher, 1941–1945

Night-planted with practised fingers,
the boy in my boxwomb
bows like a shrimp.

I train his spine to the walls,
slow as a sapling pear,
and coffin the boy in action.

I pack the boy as a present
wrapped in no room
and given to nowhere.

The boy, the boy absorbed
into a clockwork bear.
My little, traceless soft machine.

Fed piano pieces,
laboured in lies, the boy
I delivered into peace.

Rhapsody at the Cremation of a Food Writer

1

The biggest fire in firetown
they called it:

all floodlight of fat
and black bone splitpicks:

tallow-blaze
and needle-burst

bravely
blow.

The ashes, gravely,
in a white-chocolate cromlech,
kept in the fridge.

2

Out from her soke in Skibbereen,
from a fiddle hotel and the dancing sea,
pleached in her hair flies sweet Kathleen,
hugging the books of Husbandry.

Pelting through Drummanway, Durrow and Bray,
over the drink and the Dublin ferry,
Balbriggan, Drogheda, Louth and Kilrea,
and *bang!* through the Chapel of Ashes in Derry.

There in the broadside of Ph.D. Nolan
she flies at the quarks of polyphagous cud,
and takes them like orphans whose souls have been stolen
back to the air and the field and the flood.

3

Whoa, they said after
in a pint of plain,
God, I thought
it's a round with Tyson
going on in there,
treat yourself to a pew.

Wrestling with the devil,
they said, maybe,
no wonder then it took so long,
himself being so fat
as to give a fiend
a fall or two.

4

Men that book tables,
boys that plough:
where are they now?
Scattered like smoke.

5

Whilst O'Malley was asleep in the sun in front of his
butcher's shop,
I tiptoed inside and helped myself to a rather toothsome chop.

Unfortunately on the way out I trod on his espadrilles.

He awoke with a cry – aha! – and gave chase, all the while
yelling at me.
But haha I can be as nippy as your man when I want to be.

Unfortunately the swag got in the way of my oxygen.

Thus O'Malley was gaining on me lads with every stride,
and waving his bloody skewers at the treasures of my backside.

So I leapt into the Foyle and paddled doggedly towards
Coolkeeragh.

Now the waters thereabouts are pleasantly calm,
and I settled into an easy and effective overarm,

Leaving O'Malley on the distant shore execrating at the
summer air.

Imagine my surprise, then, when, being at my leisure, upon
gazing into the shining river,
I saw a dear familiar dog paddling forth carrying a darling
juicy piece of was it liver.

I shall have that, I said to myself, and showed my gums in a
very frightening manner.

Unfortunately this pye-tyke coinstantaneously did the same,
which gave me a godterrible start, and put me off my aim.

Still, I took a fair snap at his face in a colloquy of bubbles and
                                                                drool.

My only consolation is that bubblebubble down with mine
                                    his damned tucker sank.
I turned about and paddled wearily back towards the dusky bank.

The sun fell beautifully through the bridge and off the sky.

That night, the wise Jalal ad-Din Rumi came to me softly in
                                            my lovely bed.
He glided about the upper dormitory in his jubbah like your
                                        angel and said:

Do not give up the substance for the shadow bow wow.

6

> To such a chilly deadlock,
> to such a small coat,
>
> we are come.
>
> Fire diet,
> cold harvest.

Marrakesh night-tumbler

who smiles at 15 feet
aaah whaddayathink flowering
out of a twoman stalk
fitted hurray with leaves
that nnnngh and nnnngh

turns remotely up there
taraaa got up fireworkingly
glitterfizz applause and oooo
howaboutthat round and round
snailsteam fishpop souppong

yells hoha yipthings hay-yup
kerosenelamplandscape round
he claps the moon whoop wheee
the flower falls to bits slap cart
wheel clatter I beam I pay

brings thewhat thewhere the
southern cross aaaah wheeling
round and round and round huuuuge
aaah hardpalm hardsole slipslap
oh heavens yes I pay for that

Bush Baby

I'd have a wigwam
woven of wheki tow

and a moon
like a bob melon.

I'd have a cold creek
full of rippling glim

and a long ridge
from here to hang.

I'd have a bug suttee
and tap billy

and the doobs would come
for the light and bite me.

I'd climb a tightrope saddle
where the hill hangs like a puptent

and beetle over tarns
still stock still.

I'd climb through bush like scalp,
blowing at tussock and top

and breathe frost pinned
in manuka bark.

I'd climb zigzag all Mt Hopeless
and burn in the nippery sun

and the doobs would come
for the sweat and bite me.

I'd sit on a vegetable sheep,
squabbed amidst stones

and a blue lens
on a cold head.

I'd sit in a clearing, mum,
loud as the only fly

and go on, mindedly,
up, down, there and back.

I'd sit by a wheki door
half-made by the moon

and the doobs would come
for the rest and bite me.

Rak 2: Another nocturnal on St Lucy's Day
being the shortest day

This is the least light. The pointless sun
has swung its urine track behind the clouds
and gone: long men in nylon shrouds
hurry home; and everyone,
two days in front, is bright
with carelessness, and jumping guns, and light.
But this is my day: my good-as night,
whose feeble hours of yellowness decline
and die in matter's midnight land, and mine.

Let's rumble this pathetic fallacy:
Your soul is dark (last night he didn't come) –
Today's the darkest day. The sum
of *a* and *b* engenders *c*,
which is the plastic view
that Nature gives a toss; that She and you
emote *à deux*; that *a* becomes More True
as *b* is (by its Nature) cosmic/global;
that hell is, by association, Noble.

Grab your metaphysic mate and dance:
despair in lawns and truth in fallen trees,
hope in lakes and death in fleas,
carrots, camels, courage, chance,
chickens, blah blah blah.
And still the earth is dark. A purple Ka
bursts past, athud with bass; and one sick star
pricks out above the park; and next-door's cat
chucks up. What kind of metaphor is that?

He's gone. The world is big enough to find
some image in, unbloodied by the mess
of human love. I couldn't care less.
Bugger the decency of mind
over matter: today
dumps and darkness matter. Far away
a plane fights through the clouds. All Heaven's grey.
Cold, manless things, just leave me to my sorrow;
you will lighten – not my heart – tomorrow.

Midnight. Down the road the clock chimes five.
The apple-pie philosophies of art
can't save my disconnected heart,
or keep the name of love alive.
I wish we'd never met.
I wish all kinds of stuff – and yet … and yet …
The trees weep – no: the trees are dark and wet
with danky drizzle. Plastic Santas shine.
This is matter's midnight land, and mine.

Two sunburned composers

Mahler tramps all day in the hills

Hornbirds! Hoot-cuckoos!
Touch-of-the-sunburn-shivers
in heat-dappled woods.

Shostakovich goes down to the beach

Deckchair. Fags. Tarboosh.
Suit. Bowtie. Brogues. Specs. Etui.
Nose, red. Music, droll.

Go Go Gagarin Up Happy Hero

A Lensk spring nails its way
up through black boards of earth.

The school windows lie open:
tin-can rockets turn like fish on lines
caught from a cold, pea ceiling.

Outside on a moon of cracked concrete
the boys, their beaver-ears flapping,
skip like boxers in a blue detail
the brave, autistic orbits
of their whistling ropes.

Behind their heels the new grass,
unstoppable-electric-green,
launches its brutal growth.

Byelchuk, Ommon. Three pages. Good.
The light is fierce.
I know their voices, every one.

Yuri Yuri fly like fury
through the dark and endless night
bring me back a christmas cracker
give me hope and not a fright
kiss me kiss me did you miss me
out of mind is out of sight

I correct the essays of heroes.
The sky promises a fine, cold day.

How is it then, I wonder,
riding on the fuel of this spring and that,
so few escape the gravid pull of earth.

Well done. But rather short.
Yegorov, Mitiok. I put my pen aside.
I hear their boots leave the ground together:
small gods compelled to clutch at stars.
The ceiling gleams like frozen soup.

Our project Sputnik, foiled
and barely turning, dissects the room
with its knitting needles.

I walk to the windows.
The light is fierce.
I know their fathers' voices, every one.

Yuri Yuri fly like fury
through the dark and endless night
bring me back a christmas cracker
give me hope and not a fright
kiss me kiss me did you miss me
out of mind is out of sight

Les Says

Bring the bloody chooks in, Jack,
it's twenty-five below.
The frosty bush goes creak crick crack,
the hills are white with snow.

Stick them in the kitchen, Stu,
and poke the range up high.
The creek's like tin, the bracken's blue,
the sun's froze in the sky.

Dress them in my Jockeys, Mac,
and crack the bloody beers.
The roads are closed to Clyde and back.
We could be here for years.

Show them *Rocky Rooster*, Lyn,
and make them bloody laugh,
while like a chainsaw night slides in
and cuts the sun in half.

Tuck them in my bunkup, Claire,
and make them say their prayers.
Jesus, put them in my care
and don't put me in theirs.

Grandfathers

Edwin

Least likely as a spook, he dropped around
on some short, selfish day when I had lied
to shore my genes against the dark, and tried
to make me blush. 'Gidday,' I said. He frowned.
'Remember our familiar love,' he burred,
'whose short and careless warmth, unearned, unsought,
unmade, unlearned, unturned, untouched, untaught,
came like an adjective chained to the word
survival in our sentences. Goodbye.'
And that was it. A wee bit grand. But true.
I blushed. He went. He knew. I knew he knew.
There must be use in truth. I wonder why?
I went outside. The hills were cold and bright.
The moon looked kind of friendly though. Goodnight.

Josef

Most likely as a spook, he murmured down
one day when I was halfway up an Alp
and hovered in the snowy sunshine. 'Help!'
I yelled. I slipped and fell. I saw him frown.
'Of all the brave delights that I was born
to pass to you spun in my genes,' he growled,
'I'm sorry –' – tears filled up his eyes. I scowled
and scrabbled in the snow. 'Ach dear, forlorn,
distracted Man, what worm hides in the rose
of Enterprise!' I gasped. 'An unsound heart.'
He mooned away. My crampons fell apart.
Is this some kind of judgement then? God knows.
I reached the top and rested. *I* don't know.
The valleys, steeps and ridges shone with snow.

Western Man

1

Clip clop
clip clop
steady up yon stuntgrass rise, boy,
long as low and stony-brown,
slow like weeks with nothing in them:
saddle-tick,
dirt-crump,
poker-face.

Clip clop
clip clop
privy-top and anchor-wires,
church-cross, store-spike, steady boy,
up yon one-street, just more-trodden dust:
saddle-tick,
dirt-crump,
poker-face.

Clip clop
clip clop
steady, boy, through sad wood civics,
rippled in yon saloon-glass store-side,
road-end, horses maybe leaving:
saddle-tick,
dirt-crump,
poker-face.

Clip clop
clip clop
rise, boy, steady, way ahead,
purple-white mountains, nothing in them
maybe, like weeks maybe:
saddle-tick,
dirt-crump,
poker-face.

My brother's name was Crazy Sean.
They shot him in the head.
He rattled through the summer corn
and turned the green shucks red.

I laid him in the willowbrake.
I couldn't stand to pray.
I kissed his cheek for pity's sake,
and then I rode away.

The plains are full of buffalo.
The woods are red and gold.
The mountaintops are white with snow.
His memory keeps me cold.

I've rode through Hope and Whisky Creek.
I've rode through Faith and Love.
I've laid in Hate and Hide-and-Seek,
and run from God-Above.

The prairie shines, the buckdeer cry.
The hawks hang in the heat.
Clipclop clipclop, the world rolls by.
They say revenge is sweet.

Somewhere still,
Ached in long
Like a gambler's card
Vauntsquare, the nailed-up
Against the air. Clipclop –
Telegraph, clap-houses,
Into this hollow spine
O of wind. Three men
Nacarat boots, sharktooth
stark as an afternoon;
planks of sunshine;
dropped on an empty land;
main street creaks
hotel, laundry, saddles,
guns. The horse stops.
of fellowship blows a slow
clatter at a boardwalk:
mojos – oh my brother.

4

I shot one on the shithouse board. His head
smashed like a squash and sprayed the backboards red.
He pissed his boots and died. The stinking hole
spit up a fat, black fly, which was his soul.
I shot one in the barbershop. The chair
caught fire, and ate his o-colonied hair.
He fell out like a slice of spitroast meat.
The duster wrapped him in its winding-sheet.
I shot one in the cornfield. Larks of blood
flew off his skull and twittered in the mud.
He rattled through the stalks. His mashy head
threw up its brain and turned the green shucks red.
I took a bath and threw away my gun.
I rode away wherever. I was done.

5

drizzle pops on his hatbrim,
cord and wool and steam-sodden,
saddleticks like an empty stomach.

windpump wires and tin-dump,
like horizon-drowning, horse, then man,
hat, gone, clipclop, dusk drips in.

paraffin lamplight pricks the town,
glo-worms, night hunched above,
coyotes carry their eyes like stars.

6

reckoning
done
how will he ever be warm

purpose
gone
how will he outrun the storm

bearings
none
how will he find another

riding
alone
how will he tell his brother

Erdenbayat shoots a marmot

Bang!

up a small
green
bactrian
hill
the little chap
jibs
and topples

splash-in-the-grass

Chingis Dad

in memory of my father

In the Year of the Pig
the Fire of the World
went out.

I ride towards his empire.
The red-felt tongues of my boots buzz
as the engines lift us into the light
where everything is blue.

I watch the world from my window:
his conquered land looks less in the sun-up sea.

We are late amongst the glittering flotsam
sucked at his going into sudden senselessness:

where a crooked mountain
sending up a shoof of ice
through a morning sourly smelling
of meat-fat and cold, clean air
has slipped before us, and the rest –

like a life's slow, grasping explosion
reversed in a second,
and the seized ground
rebuilt in a dying flash.

We drink to the sad succession
at thirty thousand feet,
my stronger brother and I.
Under us the eye and the grain
of dad's particular harvest blow,
new-found free: the wrinkled, patched
and soul-sacked body of their shadows
is still his, like a winding-sheet
made from the skin of a mountain range.

The moonlike virgins of the moon
spill their yellow blood in every oval window.

The plane looses its freezing vapour-trail
in the freezing white air
like a fish gutted of its backbone.

Down, down, into his camp:
manuka bushes, vegetable sheep,
rocks, snow, oily parkas, kindling,
flax, keas, cold pools,
billys, tilleys, socks, tents, fires

and empty boots.
I put them on.
My brother another.

My mother another.
Their tongues are black with dubbin.
We inch into our golden gloves.

Come on then, on giant, mile-high horses,
a thousand times, a thousand times
across the freezing moss
to ruin all the earth to match his grave,
back and forth, back and forth.

A soft, sad, ski-school of ghosts slide after us:
children, grown-ups, all we've been,
strangled in the dark with blood-red scarves
so they will not tell where he is.

Above the bushline the sky fills with arrows.
Crying fires of dung and naphtha
stir the piupiu's fingers;
their silver-grey semaphores
show the way to war.

I climb alone in the still, blue snow,
like the snow I dogged his footprints in.

On the high, dead quiet,
a seam of ice glitters between the tops.

It should fall, but hangs like abstract electricity
made visible by a silver salting.

I hear the *zish zish* of his corduroys
walking like water up and up,
leaving the ridge for the clear, cold air,
like a long, aeolian whoop
that wastes on the wind.

And I am freed of pity
and of mercy and of love,
and save for the battles to come
the fierce, unkillable beauty of the world.

Mower on Mardin Gate

I met a mower sleeping on the Gate.
His scythe was pink with sunset. Way below
the Dijle, done in yellow ink, described
its name across the fields, whose pages soughed
with dying brightness. Horsemen hurried home.
The names of names went out; and then the names;
and then the world. And by its triple dark
I read my story, spun between its long,
unwritten covers, Night and Night. He snored
as light as lemonade, and teahouse tilleys
blinked and burned their sweet calligraphy
inside the city walls. I tiptoed down.
Give me love and lies. The rest is true.
And truth is dark. And night is nothing new.

At the Grave of William Bees VC

it's nice here … the Coalville sun
draws a hundred cutout doorways
easy round the lime-fizz grass:
stones, their arched unshadows, file
a hundred names in wobbled trays:
cypresses, awake with blood and bone,
twitter for birds: and all the noised
and muddled cuckoo-men on earth
are under it. The sky is cool and clean.

I like it here … the sorted shape
of baffled lives is marble-straight:
and specially here – who, caught along
the flower barbs of Time Well Spent,
deserves his round oblivion.
I hope I am so ripe when winter comes.
Heaven is a skeleton
that worked an unshot shotat man.
Sparrows sleep along the warmbrick wall.

it's nice here … the chaffless paths …
pother hoovered into peace …
oh, I've done things – but not won things:
haywire on the fields of Judgemyself,
I long for stars and stripes to take Down There.
Dragonflies arrive and stop
like unmeant bullets, gentled from these bones.
I like it here … perhaps I'll die
beyond the fight, like apples in the grass.

Two windblown painters

Caspar David Friedrich finds himself on a mountain peak

Who, pray, blew me here?
Blasé on the Sea of Clouds?
Bring my boots, Egbert!

Anwar Shemza has a smoko in his garden

Smoke scribbles away,
the leavings of ideas.
Inside – paper waits.

Anzac Snap

*'The soldier is F. Come (NZ), to be killed soon after on the crest
of Chunuk Bayir.'*

Churchill sat in a smoky chair
and watched the London rain:
We'll chase the Turks to Hell, he said,
and chase them back again.

The Beautiful Battalions sailed
under a seething sky:
they landed at Gallipoli
to do his work and die.

We'll be in Consty-nobble soon
and drinking pink champagne,
and then we'll get our medals, boys,
and sail back home again.

But X was full of dying men
and Y was full of dead,
and Heaven, boys, was full of shells
that whistled overhead.

O Johnny Turk keeps shooting, boys,
so keep your heads down low:
we'll be in Consty-nobble soon,
cos Churchill tells us so.

I just stood up to see the sea.
It's quiet, boys, I said,
and something whistled through the sky
and hit me in the head.

The farm is still at Paterau,
the sheep graze by the sea,
and men ride up and down the bush
who've never heard of me.

O History is made by men
with nothing else to do.
They watch the rain, and have ideas
to try on me and you.

But glory isn't Names and Noise,
it isn't Arms and Men:
it's living out the little life
I'll never live again.

Alien on Peddars Way

Stamping through a joke
of English greenery
I saw the future,
which was black and good.

Field and farm were glossed
with antique sunshine.
Sweetly moping furzes
cologned the mildish air.
The dreamy blueblue sky
was talcummed round
with quiet clouds.

I dipped my hobnail boots
and splashed across the tarry A11,
double-ripped like the wrong river
from made-up sweet content
to made-up sweet content
and all the sad, lime light of English art.

★

The meadow's breast is brooched
with flickered rubbish.
Seed, sap, blade, fruit,
fur, tooth, tongue, claw,
snap like plastic bags.

Here's where I saw it:
skin pricking like hot holly-leaves,
heart hopping like a scared hare.

★

Worm and seedling, weed and eye,
nature's dying: let it die.
Breath by breath and root by root,
egg and berry, paw and shoot.

Boot and beetle, tyre and track,
nature's dying: don't look back.
Stalk and twitter, jaw and flower,
inch by inch and hour by hour.

Brick and pollen, cell and sky,
nature's dying: let it die.
Wire by wire and block by block,
wing and prickle, sting and stock.

★

Tied with a rotted mother's cord
to this – damned
for sheltering the damned: we
who can make the tiger live
when god could not.

★

I cross the Thet on a bridge
like a twisted xylophone.
My boots sang.
The sun threw me
down the river.

★

When at last we're left alone
with just the things we've made:
when every stick and every bone
has dustily decayed:

when all our bright synthetics lie
like noon on Water Hill:
when nothing shakes the perfect sky
from here to Burnham Mill:

and when we're left alone at last
with just the things we need:
when Eden's fruitless hour has passed –
then we are men indeed.

Spaceman

I dreamed I came from outer space – some brown,
electric land I loved – and ran the line
from star to star, and found a world like mine.
I watched it gravely turn. I sparkled down
across the umber sea, the surge, the shore,
my country, city, streets and sheets where I,
on automatic pilot, learned to fly.
My body works without me. More and more,
the blue ideas and dreams, the killing spark,
the self-possessed, the lies, lie on my heart
to make a better man. We touch. We part.
I whizz away. My heart beats in the dark.
I woke up late and wallowed in the sun.
I know I'm fact and fiction: *I made one.*

Giant Twin Waiters at the White Cakeshop, Diyarbakır

They wait,
the mirrors say,
in icecream coatees,
everywhere:

long, yellow horseheads
ridden by multiblack
haircorps:
the sweet-salep army:

dressage-jingling
ambassadors
of the White Cakeshop
on Izzetpasha Street.

The Unknown Soldier

I'm the Unknown Soldier.
I'm buried here for good.
I died for King and Country,
like all good soldiers should.

I'm Sacrifice and Honour.
I'm Universal Love.
I'm Pity, Blood and Glory.
I sit with God Above.

My name was Johnny Suarez.
I came from Water Hill.
I fell in love one summer,
But now my heart is still.

His name was Dudsy Barrett.
He cut the reeds in Cley.
We lay in Blakeney Marshes
And watched the endless sky.

We went to fight in winter.
He died in Epernay.
So when we fought at Arras,
I threw my gun away.

My name was Johnny Suarez.
I came from Water Hill.
I fell for Dudsy Barrett,
And now my heart is still.

I'm sacrifice and glory.
I'm universal love.
I'm honour, blood and pity.
I had my god above.

Now I'm the unknown soldier.
I'm buried here for good.
I died for king and country,
Like all good soldiers should.

fellini auditions a bolognese with a very long head

i'm enchanted in this lying room
inside a blinded afternoon
that his chair ticks like
bedlegs under a child's dream

because his head is tipping its
towerblock skull into a sunbeam
electric as the memory
of canted peartrees.

Nuri and Zill

True story / Road, near Arsuz /yesterday

the sun and yet the fog
pebbles clacking with the sea
clacking with a dying echo
and I sitting smiling
poking the pebbles with my stick
saw a man I thought I knew
the sea hardly out
he u-ed like a potatopicker
u-ed and suntouched suntinted
bending gently at the pebbles
and I sitting smiling

Long ago / Road, near Arsuz / schooltime

the sun long through the windows
Zill and me listening in the sun
one lesson one subject always one
Altin Bey talking always talking
his suntouched rheumatic jaw
always one thing one lesson one subject
evolution he says feels like living he says
made to feel like living he says

not living he says and we sitting listening
smiling in the long and orange sun
and the smell of roses
woodsap in the stove
Zill and me and always the sun

Long ago / Road, near Arsuz / home

me lying spread out
under a stuffed pink satin cover
listening the tilleylamp hissing
like the sea gently rushing
lighttouched shapes sewing smoking
pink thread a line in smoke
the lightstamp of the mantel
stamped under my eyes
woodsap in the stove
and I lying smiling

*A year after / escape from Road / past the fields / no
man's land*

Road burning some war
some other war burning here
lighttouched shapes shouting running
running down behind the school
fire clacking clacking like pebbles
Altin Bey spread out in the street
stone dead dust dead
past the fields past the fire
shapes flicking and the gorse popping
popping like bubblegum
smell of roses burning
the moon high and orange

Later / no man's land / the hole

here now some hole dark blue
hidden in gorse me lying spread out
under popping gorse in the dark blue
gorse roof eyed by the moon
high and orange and still

how long who knows who cares
how long long enough

Later / the hole / dark blue

pebbles clacking the moon high and orange
someone knows someone here Zill
Zill here that's why that's all always all
one reason one lesson always one
evolution smell of roses something else
now something always something
ask why that's why that's all
long enough dark blue

Later / the hole / beyond evolution

burning world and yet the world
feels like living made to feel like
not living now beyond some other war
always some other war beyond its not
who knows who cares
how enough now enough

Later / enough

the moon high and orange
dark blue and the gorse popping
Zill opening his penknife
one lighttouched blade
always one dark blue
he cut my eye my cheek my neck my chest
my stomach my privates my legs my feet
pink threads a line through skin
always pink threads burning
popping open pitterpatter on the dead dust
rushing gently and I cutting him the same
gently with a dying echo
always the same clacking open
rushing gently with a dying echo
the lightstamp of the moon in my eyes
orange and pink

Then / the hole / who does this but you can

who does this pink satin covers
pressed together me and Zill
burning some other war pressed together
always but you can always
not living now beyond it who does this
pressed together always but you can
beyond how long who knows who cares
how long long enough
and we lying smiling
the moon high and orange
the smell of roses
the gorse popping like bubblegum

Later / Iskenderun Children's Hospital / what found us parted us

me lying spread out
under a stuffed pink satin cover me
listening always listening
the tilleylamp hissing
like the sea gently rushing always
the lightstamp of the mantel
stamped under my eyes
lighttouched shapes sewing smoking
and I lying smiling

The rest of my life / Road, near Arsuz

sixty years always sixty years
dark blue lighttouched lighttinted
the sea clacking pebbles
I poking the pebbles with my stick
u-ed like a potatopicker
clacking with a dying echo
always enough living now beyond always
and the smell of roses
and the sun long and always
and I smiling

Brother-drunk

I dress you with water
from the hose, playing
a suit of spray
from neck
to ankles.

Between cornpoles
and burned bushes
the sun clouds
your cloth
like shade.

You are drunk
by water.
It is easy to live
when needs must
wear so well.

I stitch you a suit
half glass, half smoke,
while the dropped
threads make
glaur shoes.

For as long as I keep
you clothed in rain
I am the fitter
and you are the turner
of conscience.

Already the light
stuff slows,
and you shiver.
I uncut you
and rub you dry.

Our skin is red
and peels like rep.
The corn draws in.
What we made
we can remember.

Between cool bushes
and full-dressed shucks
your shoes grow out.
We are drinking
water inside.

An Unidentified Indian from a Southeast Idaho Reservation, 1897

O cockatoony brave! My mum says, How?
Some corny CarMart sent *this* with the spiel
for BJ'S PONTIAC CHIEFTAN USED CAR DEAL –
your photo: MAKE A RESERVATION NOW,
hung up between your hands. My mum says, Shucks,
we killed 'em, son, and shakes her head. I think
that men are cruel. Their sad excuses stink.
Their God-and-Government baloney sucks.
And all their dreams are war. O Wounded Bear!
I'm not Mankind, but I apologise
for all the gimcrack glory in your eyes,
and all my savage dads that put it there:
white men who would massacre the stars
and use their names to consecrate their cars.

In Memory of Alfred Schnittke

1

Hit with a hammer   on a big blue day
Done to death   in the usual way
Swung into Heaven   on a big black swing
Knocked into Heaven where the angels sing.

2

When a traveller travelleth
through the dark forests that are near the sky
and oftentimes he is lost
and hungereth and thirsteth
and cannot see his way for anything
then hope beginneth to run away
like the sand in a glass
and the sun and its gladdening light
sinketh and fadeth
and the traveller looketh up and hurrieth on
with the heebie-jeebies and the creeps
and the darkness flickereth through the branches
and his footsteps are doubtful and doubtful
then cometh the little dark feller
who flieth and singeth where the air is thin
who is called the Long-Haired Warbler
with a little silver throat
that glittereth in the cockshut
and his feathers gleameth in the moonlight
that passeth above the shadows
and he singeth in the dark trees
and his voice is like a silver rod
that twisteth in the clouds where the sun is
and taketh the light of everything
and laughethethethethethetheth
and the traveller heareth his singing
and his heart rejoiceth down to his feet
which discovereth the heart to go on
and may findeth rest therefore
in the hut at the mountain's top.

94

This little feller thus
remindeth us of an angel
who showeth the way to the uncertain
and singeth of hope in the darkness
and giveth a hand or a wing
and the path is the path that is there
where he findeth God.

3

Must to the last, quick, living hour we come?
Cannot some sweet obstruction stay the hand
that strikes too soon: cannot the slaves be dumb
or lame that bear the news: cannot the sand
be stuck between the glasses: cannot prayers
delay the sentence: cannot Time be pricked,
misled or botched: cannot our careless heirs
give up their unlived hours and contradict
the uncontested, iron span? No no:
this greedy rage demands increase of all
the prodigal allowances we owe
for every unearned hour before our fall.
So kingly kept, so standing-long our reign,
it little recommends us to complain.

4

No simile will do: no metaphor
be half so rare: no symbol figure more
than this – borne upwards on a lime divan
by angels sweating gold, this marvellous man
ascends from cloud to cloud towards the sun,
his soul held in their hands, his business done:
the fire consumed, the God-forsaken grave,
the bright apotheosis of the brave.

5

Thou fevered, awful, too-white peak
that haunts the mind's reflection – speak!
Some say the unknown flood of thought
revolves within thy music, caught,
agleam, beyond the groaning pines
that something in the gegenschein.
Has some great something swelled thy brow
with something man knows not? Speak now!
Or is thy whirling vacancy
the something of Eternity,
whose ghastly somethings dazzle Night
and something Heaven's something light?
Thus the human mind perceives
the Sybil's answer in thy leaves
except you were a
mountain.

6

Dip the broad-winged oar and row,
Whither no man knows:
Hoist the yellow sails and go –
The high wind blows.

What fair cargo fills the hold?
No man knows its name.
Something aery, something gold –
Something like a flame.

Past the sunset come with me:
Find the way who can.
Far across the shining sea,
Take the soul of man.

7

at the third stroke
there will be no more time
my little tin Sekonda
pokes out seconds
like a boxer

in the red gym
of my heart
exactly
at the third stroke
there will be no more time

at the third stroke
there will be no more time
a plooky neon A
fizzes at gnats
like a knot
in the pink lassoo
of my brain
exactly
at the third stroke
there will be no more time

at the third stroke
there will be no more time
the wide white plain
melts in an instant
like a skin
on the green time
of my life
exactly
at the third stroke
there will be no more time

8

So be ittke
Alfred Schnittke
who have writtke
for a bittke
consumittke
composittke

9

Polly
Stylismus
est
kaput.

The muezzin who was a taperecorder

When I was young and full of prayers
I galloped up the corkscrew stairs
and threw my brimming soul away
across the rooves of Bashkale.

The minaret is strait and high
and rockets through the windy sky.
The hills are cold and bare and bright
and all the rooves are wet with light.

And now I sit below the stairs,
my youthful voice repeats its prayers
across the rooves of Bashkale
and Heaven takes my soul away.

Kabakov and the Angel

1. build me a hauntable crate such as a chicken–shed 16'9" × 7'8"
   × 6'11" (doorside) 7'2" (wallside) beams (5 × 5cm) struts (5 ×
   5cm) and door (6'3" × 2'5")

2. cover throughout with plywood hammer on beams stroke
   struts stroke door (both sides) step (5cm) and floor

3. add orbiculate doorknob

4. paint using paint white rheumy rather so plywood see 2
   shows through paint see 4 woodily giving appearance of wear
   worse for

5. enter shed

6. adjust darkness to recognise ladder planks offcuts sawhorse etc
   strewn generally about however not cluttered

7. place a stool characteristically Russian in the corner opposite entrance (door) such as might be used in a kitchen

8. fasten a lightbulb to the underside of the stoolseat having its own powersource eg a small battery the whole unseen behind the eg skirts of the stool but illuminating brightly oh brightly the area beneath the stool but not generally the shed at all

9. affix in the area at floor level the corners of which are the 4 legs of the stool and which is illuminated brightly by the concealed light a landscape characteristically Russian though not necessarily therefore unlike another see below 10

10. make this landscape out of what you will for the importance lies in its relieved (a) river flowing bluely with tiny wavelets stroke currents between (b) sandy banks steep but shortly yellow giving onto (c) hilly earth with trees stroke forests green and bushy amongst which stand (d) little houses mostly along the sandy banks generally redrooved whitewashed but not necessarily and somewhere amongst them a (e) church belltower can be seen rising but only gently from the little huddled rooves and all this bathed brightly oh brightly in the light of the lightbulb fastened to the underside of the stoolseat

11. add the angel
> with shaking fingers whose coarse
> nubs of skin and corrugated prints
> tremble at the cotton as they bluntly
> knot the end around the batterywire
> I add the angel here and sellotape
>
> I keep the angel in my palm the cotton
> drops its curl from top to bottom
> he is wood painted gold the light dull
> but golden on his shoulders hands and feet
> his wire-and-tinfoil wings flick off shadows
>
> I lower him halfway between lightbulb
> and belltower and let go the cotton turns
> and back and turns and back he's still
> descending hovering brightly oh brightly and
> the river blue he swings a little the land sways

I stand up step back the bright cube
yellows the stoolstruts the world is good
I walk backwards through the ladder
planks offcuts sawhorse etc and reach
the door which I close mostly leaving it ajar

the angel smaller than a gold flea
stays unmoved in its benevolent brightness
it has come this far there is no need
of more if I have made a memory
you are lucky if I have made hope I am glad

Meeting Ed Hilary

Aoraki's paper-crumpled peak
shoots its shadow after me.
Stapled to its glittering glacier with crampons,
hooked up to my fleshandblood with rope,
I meet Ed –

by a blue crevasse: its prehistoric
glassy crawl contends with his handshake –
hairy, warm, short, bright, brown and brave.
Then I'm cold.

Three frozen novelists

Yashar Kemal surveys the snowy Chukurova

One sheet over all.
Pricking the white world, one man –
who I love – living.

Cormac McCarthy talks with careless Nature

Snow's come. I know it.
Yonder. Leave it lay. Yessir.
It don't make a damn.

Proust feels a cold wind between lunches

Between the Rue Snob
and Honnête's private carriage,
it stings. I note this.

I tracked down the doctor who had been the last person to say goodbye to Laika in time to hear a few rambling reminiscences before he died in the TV lounge of the Old People's Home in Sestroresk

I haven't blinked for forty years.
The chairs are candy green.
Dramamine
and tears.

Ssh. The TV makes me cry.
The earth is on tonight,
blue and bright.
Goodbye.

Round and round the Quiet Room,
past a pearly – past a –
faster faster –
boooooom!

Floating on a pair of cushions,
greenly disappearing,
tiny, cheering
Rooshians.

O what weightless wonder when we
tumble, tongue-tied, whirl,
you lucky girl,
you're free.

And oh my heart is starved with pain –
no where, no air, no help,
bow-wow, yelp-yelp,
in vain.

My eyes go dim, and wherefore, why,
I never blink to see
my heart set free
to die.

The chair re-entered where he fell,
the blue world turned and turned
the bones and burned
like hell.

I paid to have his soul cremated.
It doggedly defied
the flames. I cried
and waited.

Amputeen

I hurried home with a paperbagful of hardboiled eggs.
Silvery rain dropped on the skin of Diyarbakır –
rooves, parks, awnings, gates, domes, streets.
The eggs rubbed on my pants, bugeyed, maroon and waxy.

A wet stork, dipping, watched my head hesitating on a high
                                                    pavement.
Two car-roof and horse-head currents rattled the road
through a mist of mud shot with glittering pins of aerials.
Others dived in. I cradled my eggs but dared not cross.

A bus faltered, throwing its windscreen drops forward in a
                                              whispering broadside.
In that flash, the amputeen tossed his trunk down into the traffic.
Hooves, tyres, bumpers o-ed and arched, gobbling the air in
                                                            front.
I squeezed my paperbag. A red egg bulbed slowly out –

crack – The white, crackled gap filled with zigs of silvery rain.
His ragballed hands, picking places like a fastforward flyweight,
punched the mud, here-there, there-here-there,
fight-worn, insupplicant, rubber-tough.

The stork, banking, saw his yellow gloves batter, stutter, stop.
Between threads of rain his prickled haircut vaulted
at the high pavement. I put out my hand, which he left.
The eggs spilled out of their paperbag. He boxed away.

I saw him again on a hot, purple night
with a wide, lemon moon, his head down there,
asleep against two wooden doors at the Great Mosque.
I was out for a think. The world was closed.

His haircut bristled, defiant and busy, even in sleep. Next,
a shuttered book-cart, like a dug square to the moon. And next,
a scent-cart shining glassed colours out of its lattice
at whatever looked down. I looked for a minute.

The Man Who Went the Other Way Down the Golden Road to Samarkand

It must have been another life,
but I remember I met them oh
somewhere on the road between Qasr-E-Shirin and
                                          Chah-I-Surkh.
I trotted backwards with them for a while for company
and wondered at their purpose.

I dozed on the sofa.
My book slipped.
My soul wound out of my mouth
like a white shirt in a breeze

and wished me away.
I asked them:
'Such a big, bundled, bouncing, bell-banging bunch;
where, pray, have you come from?'

And they answered:
'From Old Baghdad the Beautiful, Fat Sir:
upon the spicy, rose-drenched sniff of night
some fortnight since, we saw the Heavens stir,
and left the dim-moon city of delight.'

'I'm from Darham Muminggen Lianheqi,' I said.
They bounced along. The dust burned overhead.

We rode through a hole in the world.
Spunky's mane blew like fingers over his eyes.
I tucked in my jubbah round the saddle.
Long, long shadows rippled across the tamarisk scrub,
fandangled with camel-bells.

I sighed in a cushion.
My book fell on the rug.
My round reflection trod water
through the window

and fished me out.
I asked them:
'To what land, gentlemen, do you so eagerly ride,
with your bazaarable baggage and your soft, sedulous eyes?'

And they said:
'Hastened forth by budging hope, Fat Friend,
across the blue beyond, the boundless sand,
from wonted hearths towards the unseen end,
we take the Golden Road to Samarkand.'

'I'm on my way to Zarqa to visit my sister,' I replied.
The round horizon waited, white and wide.

I tugged at Spunky's bit. Froth chomped from his tombstone
                                              teeth
and flew forwards like lace in the braking air.
The caravan began slowly to overtake us,
rolling with more purpose and delights than we were,
contrariwise, and jingled, and bundled, and burned.

I snorted at the paper light.
My book slept
with its wings laid softly flat.
My finger tickled the hairy rug

and twitched me off.
I asked them:
'Tell me, kind sirs, what lies so chockablock
and bell-behung in all that creaking cargo?'

And they replied:
'Have we not, Fat Brother, rose-tinct jams,
wigwams, amber clams and cloud-light rice,
pungent spices, turbans, bourbons, hams,
and pekes and peacocks fit for Paradise?'

'I have a Camel-Turd Fuel-Brick Maker,' I said.
The lovely land of Zarqa retreated overhead.

They slipped athwart us flat out at the sunset,
which bobbed and bled like a barbecued tomato
about to burst through the trembling muslin of the horizon.
We stopped. Spunky rattled his mane and puffed.
I twisted and turned, unfinished, in the saddle.

I couldn't quite get comfortable.
The tip of my soul, grown and knotted
like a prisoner's escape,
fluttered at the keyhole

and fetched me through.
I asked them:
'O fast and furiously fading friends;
what fans your fiery purpose to go on?'

And they sang:
'Perhaps beyond the last, long-dreaming day
there lives a prophet who can understand
why men are born. Farewell, Fat Soul! Away!
We make the Golden Journey to Samarkand!'

And they were gone. 'Gee up, Spunky,' I said.
Behind us the bandage of the horizon stained blood-red.